This book is to be returned on
the last date stamped b

12 DEC 2007

LOCATION | M

LIBREX —

EVIDENCE IN
HISTORY
Blackie

EVIDENCE IN HISTORY

GENERAL EDITORS:
Stephen R. Gibbons
Head of Combined Studies
College of Sarum St Michael
Salisbury

Stanley J. Houston
Head of History
King's College School
Wimbledon

© David Lunn 1979
First published 1979

ISBN 0 216 90740 3

All Rights Reserved
No part of this publication may be reproduced,
stored in a retrieval system or transmitted,
in any form or by any means, electronic,
mechanical, photocopying, recording or otherwise,
without prior permission of
Blackie & Son Limited

PUBLISHED BY:
Blackie & Son Limited
Bishopbriggs, Glasgow G64 2NZ
Furnival House, 14–18 High Holborn, London WC1V 6BX

PRINTED IN GREAT BRITAIN BY:
Robert MacLehose & Co. Limited, Printers to the University of Glasgow

Preface

This series, intended for use in college courses and at GCE Advanced level, seeks actively to involve students with historical evidence. Each book provides a wealth of contemporary material for study; this material will not only illustrate many aspects of the period under study, but will also face students with some of the problems which begin to arise whenever original source material is used.

In each book questions are posed which are basic to the period concerned. The documents which follow are intended to be read with the questions in mind, and they will begin to suggest possible answers. Inevitably, they will also confront the reader with many further questions, with apparent contradictions, with problems of bias, of lack of clarity, and of interpretation – in short, with the complexity of historical judgments. The student should thus gain insights into the period under study, into the type of original material available for the study, and into the task of the historian.

This volume sets Charles II, one of the most popular and, at the same time, one of the most enigmatic of British monarchs, against the background of his times.

Stephen R. Gibbons
Stanley J. Houston
General Editors

Author's note: All dates in this volume are given according to the old style of reckoning used in England at the time, but for the sake of convenience, the year is cited in the new or Gregorian style, as beginning on 1 January, not 25 March.

Contents

1 The Restoration — 1

2 Foreign Policy 1664–1672 — 17

3 Politics 1678–1681 — 28

4 Religion — 45

5 The Economy — 53

6 Science, the Arts and Society — 62

7 Conclusions — 75

Further Reading — 89

The Restoration 1

What did the Restoration of 1660 restore?

Definitions

Not the least of the problems attending the Restoration was the definition of terms, especially since it was probably not recognized as a problem at the time. 'Restoration' can mean the giving back of something that has been stolen, in which sense the kingdom was given back to Charles II. This is the sense indicated by Dr Johnson, who, as late as 1775, hoped for a restoration of the Stuarts, whose crown had, in 1714, following the death of Queen Anne, been forced upon that reluctant Hanoverian, George I:

> George the First knew nothing, and desired to know nothing; did nothing, and desired to do nothing; and the only good thing that is told of him is that he wished to restore the crown to its hereditary successor.
>
> THE LIFE OF JOHNSON, vol. 2
> by James Boswell, edited by G. B. Hill   O.U.P., 1934–1950   p.342

But 'restoration' can also mean the attempt to bring something back to its original state by repairing it, in which sense the monarchy was restored to England, making it a complete kingdom again. The problem was that no one knew who got more out of the Restoration: King or country. Moreover, England was like a palimpsest: a manuscript whose original writing has been partly effaced in order to make way for more. How could a monarchy be restored to its original state without taking into account all that had happened – much of it of enduring value – in the previous twenty years of Civil War, regicide, Parliamentary rule and military dictatorship? It was an almost impossible situation, and the sources present conflicting evidence on the degree to which Charles and his ministers succeeded in coping with it.

First reactions

From the start, reactions differed. On the one hand, there was the unalloyed joy of the mass of the people. Since they were unrepresented in Parliament, their opinions were unimportant at the time, and historians have given them little attention. But recent research has emphasized the neutrality of the vast majority of Englishmen, who, like the dying Mercutio, invoked 'A plague o' both your houses!' on all the political and religious zealots who had made life miserable for them. John Evelyn witnessed the reaction:

> ... a triumph of above 20,000 horse and foot, brandishing their swords and shouting with inexpressible joy; the ways strawed with flowers, the bells ringing, the streets hung with tapestry, fountains running with wine; the Mayor, Aldermen and all companies in their liveries, chains of gold, banners; lords and nobles, cloth of silver, gold and velvet, every body clad in; the windows and balconies all set with ladies; trumpets, music and myriads of people flocking the streets even so far as from Rochester . . .
> JOHN EVELYN: DIARY, VOL. 3
> *edited by E. S. de Beer   O.U.P., 1955*   *p.246*

A different view was taken by Bishop Gilbert Burnet, looking back on his own times with the gloomy relish of a Scottish undertaker:

> With the restoration of the king a spirit of extravagant joy being spread over the nation, that brought on with it the throwing off the very professions of virtue and piety: all ended in entertainments and drunkenness, which overran the three kingdoms to such a degree, that it very much corrupted all their morals. Under the colour of drinking the king's health, there were great disorders and much riot every where.
> HISTORY OF MY OWN TIME, vol. 1
> *edited by O. Airy   O.U.P., 1897–1900*   *pp.165–166*

Amidst the general rejoicings, the King was heard to make the sardonic and characteristic aside,

> that it could be nobody's fault but his own that he had stayed so long abroad when all mankind wished him so heartily at home.
> CHARLES II
> *by K. H. D. Haley   The Historical Association, 1966*   *p.12*

On the other hand, the 'political nation' – composed of those who had sufficient property to qualify them for representation in Parliament – were more cautious. According to Macaulay, a Whig, who based his history on their views,

> the great body of the nation leaned to the Royalists. The crimes of Strafford and Laud, the excesses of the Star Chamber and of the High Commission, the great services which the Long Parliament had, during the first year of its existence, rendered to the state, had faded from the minds of men. The execution of Charles the First, the sullen tyranny of the Rump, the violence of the army, were remembered with loathing; and the multitude was inclined to hold

Bust of Charles II by Honore Pellé

all who had withstood the late King responsible for his death and for the subsequent disasters.

The House of Commons, having been elected while the Presbyterians were dominant, by no means represented the general sense of the people. Most of the members, while execrating Cromwell and Bradshaw, reverenced the memory of Essex and of Pym. One sturdy Cavalier who ventured to declare that all who had drawn the sword against Charles the First were as much traitors as those who had cut off his head, was called to order, placed at the bar, and reprimanded by the Speaker. The general

wish of the House undoubtedly was to settle the ecclesiastical disputes in a manner satisfactory to the moderate Puritans. But to such a settlement both the court and the nation were averse.
THE HISTORY OF ENGLAND FROM THE ACCESSION OF JAMES II, vol. I
by Lord Macaulay, edited by C. H. Firth   Macmillan, 1911 pp.145–146

When the possibility of a restoration became apparent, it was soon clear that the chief powerbrokers in England – men who had opposed both Charles I and Cromwell impartially – would make it difficult, if not impossible, to restore the past completely, either to the pre-1640 situation, when Charles I had ruled unfettered by Parliament, or to some mythical earlier age of 'Tudor harmony'. Such a restoration would have been a revolution: the overthrow of twenty years' achievements. In the Declaration which he made at Breda in April 1660, like an election manifesto, Charles showed that he was aware of the underlying problems unenvisaged by the mass of the people:

> If the general distraction and confusion which is spread over the whole kingdom doth not awaken all men to a desire and longing that those wounds which have so many years together been kept bleeding, may be bound up, all we can say will be to no purpose; however, after this long silence, we have thought it our duty to declare how much we desire to contribute thereunto . . .
>
> And to the end that the fear of punishment may not engage any . . . we do, by these presents, declare, that we do grant a free and general pardon, which we are ready, upon demand, to pass under our Great Seal of England, to all our subjects, of what degree or quality soever, who, within forty days after the publishing hereof, shall lay hold upon this our grace and favour, and shall, by any public act, declare their doing so, and that they return to the loyalty and obedience of good subjects; excepting only such persons as shall hereafter be excepted by Parliament, those only to be excepted. . . .

From PUBLIC RECORDS OFFICE; STATE PAPERS 18/221, fol.4
quoted in LETTERS, SPEECHES AND DECLARATIONS OF KING CHARLES II
edited by Sir A. Bryant   Cassell, 1935   *p.84*

By contrast, Charles's speech to the Lords on his arrival in London a month later seemed to contain a delicate hint that he had enough popular support to enable him to stand up to the politicians:

> MY LORDS,
>
> I am so disordered by my journey, and with the noise still sounding in my ears (which I confess was pleasing to me, because it expressed the affections of my people), as I am unfit at the present to make such a reply as I desire. Yet thus much I shall say unto you, that I take no greater satisfaction to myself in this my change, than that I find my heart really set to endeavour by all

Charles II's reception in London: detail from 'Charles II's Coronation Procession' *by Dirck Stoop*

means for the restoring of this nation to their freedom and happiness; and I hope, by the advice of my Parliament, to effect it. Of this also you may be confident, that, next to the honour of God, from whom principally I shall ever owe this Restoration to my Crown, I shall study the welfare of my people, and shall not only be a true Defender of the Faith, but a just assertor of the laws and liberties of my subjects.

JOURNALS OF THE HOUSE OF LORDS, 1660–1666   p.48

The new King

The chief architects of the Restoration settlement were Charles himself and Edward Hyde, later Earl of Clarendon, his chief adviser in exile. Opinions differ about the personality and competence of both men. Charles was and is one of the most popular – and most criticized – of English monarchs; one of the best known, and most enigmatic. Historians have wrangled over his reputation like the doctors who treated his dying body so atrociously; likewise, schoolmasterish contemporaries, praising his potential while they belittled his performance; censorious nineteenth-century Whigs; and, in our own age, severe academics, Tory biographers and a host of popular writers. The following extracts, along with those in the final chapter of this book, attempt to present a full picture of Charles, and the contrasting lights in which he is viewed. Was he simply the hireling of a despotic foreign king – or a master of diplomacy? A bad manager of Parliament – or the most skilful politician of his age? A butterfly mind – or a discerning patron of art, literature, music, architecture and science? An irresponsible spendthrift – or a determined promoter of England's commercial prosperity? In short, a lazy, disillusioned rake, untrustworthy, unscrupulous, unloving and unmourned – or a great statesman, wit, lover and sportsman? In a poem attributed to Andrew Marvell, the author made what appeared to be a laudatory comparison between Charles and Saul, King of the Israelites, though perhaps a satirical tone may be detected:

John Wilmot, 2nd Earl of Rochester by Jacob Huysmans

> Of a tall stature, and of sable hue,
> Much like the son of Kish, that lofty Jew,
> Twelve years complete he suffered in exile,
> And kept his father's asses all the while.
>
> ANDREW MARVELL: COMPLETE WORKS, vol. I
> *edited by A. B. Grosart   Privately printed, 1872–1875*   p.343

John Wilmot, Lord Rochester, was more direct:
> Here lies a great and mighty king,
> Whose promise none relies on;
> He never said a foolish thing,
> Nor ever did a wise one,

to which Charles replied:
> My words are my own, but my acts are my ministers'.
>
> LORD ROCHESTER'S MONKEY
> *by Graham Greene   Bodley Head, 1974*   p.88

Professor Andrew Browning, on the other hand, has written:
> Charles was at his best in the early years of his reign. He interfered little in affairs, behaved with great dignity in a difficult situation, and by his immense personal charm helped to soothe the susceptibilities of the innumerable representatives of all parties who felt they were being neglected or ill used. As son and heir of the 'Royal Martyr' he had it in his power to exercise a greater influence than anyone else on the general tone of the settlement, and he used that influence almost entirely for good. Without seeming in any way neglectful of his father's memory he yet threw his weight on the side of moderation, and it was largely due to him that so little blood was shed on the scaffold, and that the Act of Indemnity and Oblivion, granting an amnesty for nearly all offences of the previous eighteen years, was eventually passed.

ENGLISH HISTORICAL DOCUMENTS, vol. 8 (1660–1714)
edited by A. Browning   Eyre & Spottiswoode, 1953   *p.4*

Clarendon

It is difficult to reconcile conflicting opinions about Clarendon. On the one hand, he was said to have been
> honest, resolute and indefatigable . . . had once himself been an opponent of Charles I, and had enough sympathy with both sides in the original quarrel to be able to act as mediator between them. The land settlement embodied in the Act of Indemnity and Oblivion, which required the restoration of all land confiscated by the Government, but recognized all sales by legitimate owners, even when effected under practical duress, was the offspring of his practised legal mind, and, however inequitable, caused less upheaval and discontent than any other solution of the problem would have done. The Church settlement was in general accordance with his ideas, though the name 'Clarendon Code', given to the series of statutes recognizing the supremacy of the Anglican communion and depressing its rivals, conveys an exaggerated impression of the length to which he wished to go. Most important of all, the constitutional settlement, with its insistence on the supremacy of the law, and its conception of king and Parliament as substantially equal powers working harmoniously together, was due primarily to him. His enemies among the discontented Cavaliers later declared that he had deliberately frustrated every attempt to provide the king with a sufficient revenue to make him independent, and though there seems to be no real foundation for the charge, it is not altogether out of keeping with his general policy. To Clarendon and, under his guidance, to Charles, restoration meant a return to the position obtaining in the spring of 1642, and for that conception of restoration there was almost

certainly more support in the country at large than there would have been for any other.
ENGLISH HISTORICAL DOCUMENTS, vol. 8 (1660–1714)
edited by A. Browning   Eyre & Spottiswoode, 1953   *p.5*

On the other hand, his contemporary, Burnet, was more severe:
> ... he spoke too copiously; he had a great pleasantness in his spirit, which carried him sometimes too far into raillery, in which he sometimes showed more wit than discretion. He went over to the Court party when the war was like to break out, and was much in the late king's councils and confidence during the war. ... he was a man that knew England well, and was lawyer good enough to be an able Chancellor, and was certainly a very incorrupt man. In all the king's foreign negotiations he meddled too much, for I have been told that he had not a right notion of foreign matters; but he could not be gained to serve the interests of other princes. Mr. Fouquet sent him over a present of 10,000 pounds after the king's restoration, and assured him he would renew that every year; but though both the king and the duke advised him to take it he very worthily refused it. He took too much upon him and meddled in everything, which was his greatest error.

HISTORY OF MY OWN TIME; SUPPLEMENT
edited by H. B. Foxcroft   O.U.P., 1902   *pp.53–55*

Clarendon's character, as shown in this exchange of notes between him and Charles at the Council table, may have had something to do with his unpopularity:
> *Chas.* I would willingly make a visit to my sister at Tunbridge for a night or two at farthest, when do you think I can best spare that time?
>
> *Clar.* I know no reason why you may not for such a time, [2 nights] go the next week, about Wednesday, or Thursday, and return time enough for the adjournment; which yet ought to be the week following. I suppose you will go with a light Train.
>
> *Chas.* I intend to take nothing but my night bag.
>
> *Clar.* Yes. You will not go without 40 or 50 horse.
>
> *Chas.* I count that part of my night bag.

From Notes Which Passed at Meetings of The Privy Council
quoted in LETTERS, SPEECHES AND DECLARATIONS OF KING CHARLES II
edited by Sir A. Bryant   Cassell, 1935   *p.104*

The land settlement

Clarendon's unpopularity alone, however, cannot account for his downfall in 1667. There were a number of disasters, such as the Dutch attack up the Medway, for which he was made a scapegoat. But there were also the continuing problems of the Restoration, one of which was

Edward Hyde, Earl of Clarendon

the question of how to settle the property of Royalists which had been bought after confiscation and had, in many cases, changed hands more than once. It seemed too tangled a problem, although Charles's Declaration of Breda implied that he thought it could be solved:

> And because, in the continued distractions of so many years, and so many and great revolutions, many grants and purchases of estates have been made to and by many officers, soldiers and others, who are now possessed of the same, and who may be liable to actions at law upon several titles, we are likewise willing that all such differences, and all things relating to such grants, sales and purchases, shall be determined in Parliament, which can best provide for the just satisfaction of all men who are concerned.

From PUBLIC RECORDS OFFICE; STATE PAPERS 18/221, fol. 4
quoted in LETTERS, SPEECHES AND DECLARATIONS OF KING CHARLES II
edited by Sir A. Bryant   Cassell, 1935   *p.84*

However, Parliament's Act of Indemnity **and Oblivion**, which was partly designed to settle property disputes, at least in principle, became the occasion of satire, as is shown in this newsletter of 30 June 1660:

> Some unhappy wit, amongst other queries scattered in a paper in the Privy Chamber, made one whether it were not fit His Majesty should pass an Act of Indemnity for his enemies and of Oblivion for his friends.

LETTERS, SPEECHES AND DECLARATIONS OF KING CHARLES II
edited by Sir A. Bryant   Cassell, 1935   *p.98*

Curiously enough, this remark echoed a debate that had taken place before the Restoration on whether it was more advisable to reward enemies than friends. The argument hinged on how strong were those who now possessed Royalists' lands, since if they were too strong, the Restoration itself might never happen. General Monck took the more pessimistic view:

> Before these unhappy wars the government of these nations was monarchical in church and state. These wars have given birth to several interests both in church and state heretofore not known, though now upon many accounts very considerable, as the Presbyterian, Independent, Anabaptist, and sectaries of all sorts, as to ecclesiastics, and the purchasers of the King's, Queen's, Princes', bishops', deans' and chapters' and all other forfeited estates, and all these engaged in these wars against the king as to civils. . . . If this being so, then the government under which we formerly were, viz. monarchy, cannot possibly be admitted for the future in these nations because its support is taken away, and because it is exclusive of all the former interests both civil and spiritual, all of them being incompatible with monarchical uniformity in church and state thus expired. That government then that is best able to comprehend and protect all interests, as is aforesaid, must needs be republick.

From A Register and Chronicle Ecclesiastical and Civil, 1728 by White Kennett
quoted in THE RESTORATION
by Joan Thirsk   Longman, 1976   *pp.83–84*

On the other hand, the Duke of Newcastle, an old-fashioned Royalist, had this advice for the King:

> Now, Sir, with your Majesty's favour, I will speak of the greatest error of state that ever was committed in these two last reigns and that is, that they ever rewarded their enemies, and neglected their friends. . . . This was but a weak policy to take off enemies. Nay, they would say: he was a shrewd man, we must please him, reward him, make him a lord, give him office. But for a friend, he is an honest man, give him nothing, he'll do us no hurt. Certainly, this

policy was brought out of the Indies, where they pray to the Devil and not to God, for they say God's a good man, and will do nobody hurt. Therefore, they will pray and flatter the Devil that may hurt them.
Bodleian Library, Oxford; Clarendon MSS 109, fol. 60
quoted in THE RESTORATION
by Joan Thirsk Longman, 1976 *p.3*

How much truth, then, was there in the satire about the Act of Indemnity and Oblivion? Edward Hyde believed that the Act ought to embrace friend and enemy alike without exception, in order to prevent further dispute:

His Majesty well knows that, by this Act, he hath gratified and obliged many worthy and pious men who have contributed much to his Restoration.... but he is not so sure that he may not likewise have gratified some who did neither contribute to his coming in, nor are yet glad that he is in.
From The Parliamentary History of England, 1808, vol. 4, by William Cobbett
quoted in THE RESTORATION
by Joan Thirsk Longman, 1976 *p.5*

Lord Ailesbury, writing many years later, saw in this Act the origins of the Whig or Parliamentarian party:

'Whiggism' ... really sprung by degrees from the discontent of noble families and of many good families of the first gentry in the counties whose ancestors were sequestered, decimated, and what not on account of their steadfast loyalties.... The noble historian [Clarendon] could never give the Earl of Derby scarce one good word in his history, and crowned his dislike at the Restoration towards my lord, his son, and my lady, his mother, in advising my good king and master to give the negative to that bill [restoring the Earl of Derby to his lands], ... and for why? To favour Sergeants Maynard and Glyn, etc., who came to that lord's part of estate so unjustly and inhumanly.
From Lord Ailesbury: Memoirs, vol. 1
quoted in THE RESTORATION
by Joan Thirsk Longman, 1976 *p.7*

Professor J. P. Kenyon, however, is more generous:

The Act of Indemnity and Oblivion is a remarkable document; with the exception of those who had signed Charles I's death warrant or officiated at his execution, plus a few particularly obnoxious individuals, like Vane, Lambert and Haslerigg, everyone received a full pardon, and all process of revenge or retribution was halted. More remarkable still, for three years penalties were

imposed for reflecting, by speech or writing, on any man's conduct during the past twenty years.
THE STUART CONSTITUTION
by J. P. Kenyon   C.U.P., 1966   *p.362*

Parliamentary legislation on land restoration was not final, however, as these notes passed between Charles and Clarendon suggest:

Chan.   I think it is but just to give my Lord Worcester such papers as may manifest his debt. I tell them the trunk is in your custody, because I will not suffer my Lord Worcester to look into it, therein being many papers he should not have, which were signed by your father; but what concerns his account of moneys disbursed by him for your father, he ought to have, and I shall deliver them to him, if you please, as soon as I can get time to peruse them. And then you may consider of the forty thousand pounds.
King.   Let my Lord Worcester have his accounts and papers to that purpose, which I doubt not but will bring forth a new cheat.
Chan.   As troublesome as you take him to be, he is an angel in comparison of his wife, and his brother John, who torment me every day to get them forty thousand pounds upon this warrant from my Lord Worcester which you have read.
From Notes Which Passed at Meetings of The Privy Council
quoted in LETTERS, SPEECHES AND DECLARATIONS OF KING CHARLES II
edited by Sir A. Bryant   Cassell, 1935   *p.84*

The final verdict on the economic results of the land settlement must be left to a later chapter, but in the meantime there is Joan Thirsk's conclusion:

Seventy per cent of the properties which were sold under the Commonwealth in southeastern England have been traced back to their owners in 1660, and further enquiry would probably yield more. Thus, forty-five out of 179 estates were recovered before 1660, and at least 81 afterwards. Royalists regained their land in all but exceptional circumstances.
THE RESTORATION
by Joan Thirsk   Longman, 1976   *p.98*

Historians, using such texts and weighing up the circumstances, have to decide whether anything better – a planned economic reconstruction, rather than a restoration – could have been attempted, such as, two centuries later, America attempted after her Civil War. Certainly, England needed such a reconstruction:

Underlying everything else was a strong undercurrent of economic unrest. Prices had long been rising, and though the process had by this time virtually ceased, the necessary readjustment on a new

level had not yet taken place. All classes complained that their expenditure had increased, but shut their eyes to the fact that their income had usually done so too. War and revolutionary ideas between them had shattered the social fabric. Large numbers of men had abandoned the occupations to which they had been brought up, and either could not or would not return to them. Land in very considerable amounts had changed owners. The stable England of the earlier part of the seventeenth century had vanished, and a long process of reconstruction, not just some magic 'restoration', was to prove necessary before stability could again be attained.
ENGLISH HISTORICAL DOCUMENTS, vol. 8 (1660–1714)
edited by A. Browning   Eyre & Spottiswoode, 1953   *p.4*

Religious restoration

One of Charles's promises in the Declaration of Breda was:
And because the passion and uncharitableness of the times have produced several opinions in religion, by which men are engaged in parties and animosities against each other (which, when they shall hereafter unite in a freedom of conversation, will be composed or better understood), we do declare a liberty to tender consciences, and that no man shall be disquieted or called in question for differences of opinion in matter of religion, which do not disturb the peace of the kingdom; and that we shall be ready to consent to such an Act of Parliament, as, upon mature deliberation, shall be offered to us, for the full granting that indulgence.
From PUBLIC RECORDS OFFICE; STATE PAPERS 18/221, fol. 4
quoted in LETTERS, SPEECHES AND DECLARATIONS OF KING CHARLES II
edited by Sir A. Bryant   Cassell, 1935   *p.84*

The full effects of Charles's failure to implement this promise and of the religious settlement in general will be discussed in a later chapter. It must be remembered, however, that the so-called 'Clarendon Code', with its rigid emphasis on uniformity, was not Clarendon's, and that it belongs to 1662 and the years following, not to the first two years of the Restoration. Against a chorus of disapproval of the religious settlement, at least one modern writer has something positive to say about the early legislation:
... the matter is not so simply stated as Professor Clark would have us believe: 'Against the hardening bigotry of the Anglicans he [Baxter] could do nothing'. The Laudians firmly rejected the scheme of comprehension put forward by a section of the Puritans; they did not decry the ideal of comprehensiveness. On the contrary, they believed and constantly asserted that within

traditional Anglican limits a wider range of belief and practice was possible than in any other religious settlement, and later history has not disproved this claim.

THE MAKING OF THE RESTORATION SETTLEMENT
by R. S. Bosher   Dacre Press, 1957   *p.277*

The United Kingdom

Scotland and Ireland also had problems which called for urgent attention. Charles to the Earl of Middleton (Commissioner to the Parliament of Scotland), March 1660:

> I have given you a full answer to your letter. Yet one thing I must add, and it shall be to yourself. I am sorry to hear from so many hands that a strange course is taken there with many of those who were appointed to be cited to the Parliament. Private bargains I hear are driven, and money received from too many who are represented to have been abominable compliers. I shall be glad that this be not so, for although I should have been apt enough to have pardoned such as had been offered as the fittest objects of mercy, and although I was willing to leave those things very much to the Parliament, yet I did ever understand that the sole power of pardoning resides in me and that fines and forfeitures are wholly at my disposal. You shall therefore privately inform yourself if any such strange way be taken and let it be stopped. For I am clearly of opinion that pardoning and publishing is to be carried above board, and that no private bargains are to be driven to make sale of my grace and mercy. Let me, I pray you, have an account of this.

LETTERS, SPEECHES AND DECLARATIONS OF KING CHARLES II
edited by Sir A. Bryant   Cassell, 1935   *p.108*

1661

King. When will it be fit to call in the Irish as they desired last night?

Chan. Whenever you have a mind to spoil the business; really all will come to nothing if you call them in.

King. I cannot imagine, with any justice, how I can refuse to hear them since they desire it.

Chan. Have you not heard them? If you do call them, the other side must be called too, and then we are in till morning. If you are tender hearted on their behalf I pray leave them to the House of Commons, and their work is done. They are mad and do not understand their own interest. Sir Nicholas Plunkett is desperate and would make all others so too.

King. For my part, rebel for rebel, I had rather trust a Papist rebel than a Presbyterian one. . . .

*   *   *   *   *   *   *   *

King. The Irish make a complaint, methinks with reason, that my Lord Anglesey should be both party and judge.
Chan. He ought not to be, nor can when you are by.
King. I mean in the committee for Irish affairs where he may impose unreasonable things upon the rest, who are not so much concerned as he is.
Chan. My Lord Privy Seal will watch him, but I think when you have taken your resolutions in the main, that committee will not be able to do much.
King. But methinks 'tis an ugly thing for me to make a party judge.
From Notes Which Passed at Meetings of The Privy Council
quoted in LETTERS, SPEECHES AND DECLARATIONS OF KING CHARLES II
edited by Sir A. Bryant   Cassell, 1935   *pp.108–109*

Professor Browning's view:
Unfortunately neither Charles nor Clarendon appreciated the fact that the admirable principles which they supported in England could with equal advantage be observed in Scotland and Ireland, and that it might be worth their while, in the interests of all three kingdoms, to do what they could to promote a similar moderation and readiness to compromise there. As a result the restoration in Scotland was encouraged to go much too far, while the restoration in Ireland was prevented from going nearly far enough, in each case because that was the course which seemed most in consonance with the immediate interests of England. Despite the lessons plainly embodied in the events of the previous twenty years, English statesmen still failed to realize that the three kingdoms of the British Isles were inseparably connected together, and that the interests of one could not be promoted by ignoring the interests of the others. Their selfish and short-sighted policy in this particular was to be one of the main causes of the very unrest which all were so anxious to bring to an end.
ENGLISH HISTORICAL DOCUMENTS, vol. 8 (1660–1714)
edited by A. Browning   Eyre & Spottiswoode, 1953   *p.5*

Conclusion

A balanced conclusion on the value of the Restoration can only be attempted at the end of this book. 'The truth is seldom pure and never simple', said Oscar Wilde, but at the time Blaise Pascal, musing whimsically on the miraculous, seemed rather more sure:
Cromwell was about to ravage all Christendom, the royal family was undone, and his own forever established save for a little grain of sand which formed in his ureter. Rome herself was trembling under him, but this small piece of gravel having formed, there he is

Whitehall Palace by Visscher

dead, his family cast down, all is peaceful, the King restored.
From Fact and Fancy in 1660 by C. Robbins
quoted in THE RESTORATION OF THE STUARTS, BLESSING OR DISASTER?
Huntingdon Library Publications, 1958

Historians disagree about what was restored and how effectively: a strong monarchy – hampered by Parliament; the Church of England – cut off from a large number of Englishmen; liberty – or repression. Professor Andrew Browning argues that the settlement was an *un*settlement, since it imposed no actual restraints on the monarchy and thus allowed ideas of absolutism to get into the heads of Charles II and later James II. The only real settlement, he argues, came with the latter's downfall in 1688 and the establishment of cut-and-dried rules for the relationship of King and people. For the failure of the Restoration he places much of the blame on Clarendon:

> Clarendon's real weakness, however, was not so much selfishness or lack of foresight as an inability to appreciate the age in which he was now living. Of a naturally conservative temper, enhanced by his profession and by advancing years, he was still dominated by the ideas and ideals of the reign of Charles I.

ENGLISH HISTORICAL DOCUMENTS, vol. 8 (1660–1714)
edited by A. Browning   Eyre & Spottiswoode, 1953

Foreign Policy 1664-1672   2

Why did Charles II sign the Treaty of Dover, and what were its effects?

Charles II and the Dutch

Historians differ about the motives and effects of Charles II's foreign policy. The Whig historians, writing in the aftermath of the Napoleonic Wars, and basing themselves mainly on Parliamentarian records, saw his policy as one of weak subservience to France. Later historians, reacting against this interpretation, saw the policy as a return to the proud and aggressive tradition of Elizabeth and Cromwell, who strengthened ties with France in order to defeat the commercial rivalry, first of Spain and then of Holland. The following extracts provide some clues about Charles's attitude to the Dutch. They should be read in conjunction with the evidence in Chapter Five on Anglo-Dutch commercial rivalry.

The Dutch in the Medway, 1667:
> The Royal Charles, Sta. Maria, Royal Oak, Royal James, Loyal London, and Unity, all great ships, are burned by the Dutch in Chatham River, besides two lesser ships, wherein were 500 men, all lost, and 12 more ships sunk in the river's mouth, to prevent the enemy coming in; yet they got over them and the chain too, and did this mischief. This compelled the sinking of all the other great ships near Chatham dock, not leaving one above water, but it is hoped these will be recovered in time. The merchants are undone; the great money bankers have shut up their shops; people are ready to tear their hair off their heads; great importunity has been used at Whitehall, especially by Sir George Saville, for a Parliament, but nothing will prevail; there is one great gown man against it, also all the bishops and papists, and all those who have cozened and cheated the King. News arrives to-day that the French have come from Brest, and appear before the Isle of Wight; some at Court give out that they are friends, and not enemies. The Dutch are expected as far as Woolwich; people are fled from Greenwich and

> Blackwall with their wives and children. "We are betrayed, let it light where it will."
>
> CALENDAR OF STATE PAPERS DOMESTIC, 1667   pp.188–189

Speech in Parliament by the Earl of Shaftesbury, 5 February 1673:

> His Majesty . . . hath referred you to his declaration, where you will find the personal indignities, by pictures and medals and other public affronts, his Majesty hath received from the States; their breach of treaties both in the Surinam and East India business; and at last they come to that height of insolence as to deny the honour and right of the flag, though an undoubted jewel of the Crown, never to be parted with, and by them owned in the late treaty of Breda, and never contested in any age. . . . The King and his ministers had here a hard time, and lay every day under new obloquies. Sometimes they were represented as selling all to France for money to make this war. Portsmouth, Plymouth and Hull were to be given into the French hands for caution. . . . Then the obloquy was turned from treachery to folly. The ministers were now fools that some days before were villains. . . . But both kings, knowing their interests, resolved to join against them, who were the common enemy to all monarchies, and I may say especially to ours, their only competitor for trade and power at sea, and who only stand in their way to an universal empire as great as Rome. . . . All this you and the whole nation saw before the last war . . . that at any rate *delenda est Carthago*.
>
> JOURNALS OF THE HOUSE OF COMMONS, vol. 9   pp.246–248

Letter of Charles to his sister, Henrietta Anne, Duchess of Orléans, 27 February 1665:

> I am sorry that my Lord Holles has asked justice upon a point of honour that I should never have thought of. You know the old saying in England, the more a turd is stirred, the more it stinks, and I do not care a turd for anything a Dutchman says of me. And so I think you have enough upon this dirty subject, which nothing but a stinking Dutchman could have been the cause of. But pray thank the King, my brother, and desire him not to take any kind of notice of it, for such idle discourses are not worth his anger or mine. I have been all this day at Hampton Court, and it is so long since I have been a-horseback as with this small day's journey I am weary enough to beg your pardon if I say no more now. . . .
>
> *From Madame by Julia Cartwright, 1894*
>
> quoted in LETTERS, SPEECHES AND DECLARATIONS OF KING CHARLES II
> edited by Sir A. Bryant   Cassell, 1935   p.178

Charles II and France

The following texts show the terms on which Charles approached an alliance with France. To his favourite sister, 'Minette', he could write

'The Princess Henrietta', *attributable to Sir Peter Lely*

frankly. How great an influence was she on the determination of Charles's foreign policy? His intimate letters to her must be balanced with evidence of more hard-headed motives. His attitude, for example, to her 'prophet', the Abbé Pregnani, may show how far Charles's head was ruled by his heart, while his instructions to the Duke of York and his statement of policy to Louis indicate less than complete subservience to France. Did Charles genuinely intend to profess himself a Catholic, as he promised in the Secret Treaty of Dover? His Declaration of Indulgence was quickly dropped in the face of opposition. The effects on English politics of the Treaty are discussed in the next chapter. Meanwhile, an assessment of the evidence will help us to decide who gained most from the Treaty: England's commercial lobby, which wished to see the Dutch rivalry defeated; Louis, who bought England's help in France's war against the Dutch; or Charles, who gained money from Louis in return for – what?

Letters of Charles to Madame, 14 September 1668 and 22 March 1669:
> I came from Newmarket the day before yesterday, where we had as fine weather as we could wish, which added much both to the horse matches as well as to hunting. L'Abbé Pregnani was there most part of the time, and I believe will give you some account of it, but not that he lost his money upon confidence that the stars could tell which horse would win. For he had the ill luck to foretell three times wrong together, and James believed him so much as he lost his money upon the same score.

(The Abbé, an Italian priest with a fashionable reputation for casting horoscopes, had been sent by Louis in the hope that his predictions, inspired no doubt by Louis, would hasten Charles's public conversion to Catholicism and to France.)

> . . . you may be sure that I will continue my care to let them see the power you have over me, and how much my kindness to you adds to my inclination to live always very well with France. . . .
>
> . . . I do intend to go to Newmarket the last day of this month, at which place and at Audley End, I shall stay near a month. My wife goes to the latter of these places at the same time, which is all I will trouble with at this time but to assure you that 'tis impossible to have more kindness and tenderness than I have for you.
>
> What you sent by Mercer is lost, for there are letters come that informs of his setting sail from Havre, in an open *challoupe*, with intention to come to Portsmouth, and we have never heard of him since, so he is undoubtedly drowned. I hear Mam* sent me a present by him, which, I believe, brought him the ill luck, so as she ought, in conscience, to be at the charges of praying for his soul, for 'tis her fortune has made the man miscarry. And so, my dearest sister, I am yours, with all the kindness and tenderness imaginable.

From Madame by Julia Cartwright, 1894
quoted in LETTERS, SPEECHES AND DECLARATIONS OF KING CHARLES II
edited by Sir A. Bryant   Cassell, 1935   pp.224–226; 232–233
* 'Mam' refers to their mother, whose bad luck at sea was a family joke.

Letter of Charles to the Duke of York, 23 February 1668:
> Most dear brother, we greet you well. Whereas we have received information of great violences committed in several of our ports by certain ships under the command of the Sieur de la Roche, we have for the preventing the like for the future, as well as obtaining

satisfaction for those already done, been pleased to signify our pleasure to you, that . . . you give orders to Sir Thomas Allen, Knight, to sail towards those parts where it is probable he may find the said Sieur de la Roche, in performing of which he is carefully to observe the following instructions. He is to look for the said Sieur de la Roche in all our ports, bays and roads of this our kingdom as far as Falmouth. . . . In case he finds him in any of them, he is to come to an anchor by the said Sieur de la Roche, and if he, the said Sir Thomas Allen, judge himself the stronger so as to be able to compel him, he is to require of him immediately to deliver to him all our subjects, whether seamen or others, who are on board any of the ships under his command.

From PUBLIC RECORDS OFFICE; STATE PAPERS 29/235, fol. 55
quoted in LETTERS, SPEECHES AND DECLARATIONS OF KING CHARLES II
edited by Sir A. Bryant   Cassell, 1935   *pp.215–216*

Letter of Charles to Madame, 5 March 1668:
I received your long letter of the 7th inst. now, wherein I perceive you are very much alarmed at my condition, and at the cabals which are growing here. I do take your concern for me very kindly, and thank you for the counsel you give me, but I do not think you have so much cause to fear as you seem to do in your letter. There is no doubt but a House of Commons will be extravagant enough when there is need of them, and 'tis not much to be wondered at that I should be in debt after so expenseful a war as I have had, which undoubtedly will give me some trouble before I get out of it. I will not deny but that naturally I am more lazy than I ought to be, but you are very ill informed if you do not know that my Treasury, and indeed all my other affairs, are in as good a method as our understandings can put them into.

From Madame by Julia Cartwright, 1894
quoted in LETTERS, SPEECHES AND DECLARATIONS OF KING CHARLES II
edited by Sir A. Bryant   Cassell, 1935   *p.216*

Statement of England's position in regard to France in the event of a war with Holland, 24 January 1670:
As a war against Holland would in all respects suit with the interests of England and be very advantageous to it if the King of Great Britain had force ready to be master of the seas: so on the other hand if the Hollanders should be strongest at sea nothing in the world could be so pernicious to England as that war.

All our trade, being considerable in many stations and parts in and out of Europe, would be exposed as a prey to our enemy, and particularly that of Gothenburgh and Norway, for masts, pitch tar and the other naval provisions with which England must perpetually be supplied, will be totally interrupted, and besides the trade of our plantations the plantations themselves would be in danger to be lost if there be not a naval force subsisting there to relieve them.

Beyond this, the affront to the nation of the Dutch laying upon our unfortified coasts and blocking up our open rivers would not be borne without a danger of mutinies and universal disorders, or if they should not happen the interruption only of the trade would cut off one of the best branches of His Majesty's revenue, viz., the customs valued at 500,000 sterling yearly, and this at a time when His Majesty would have most need of money. By this it is evident that the King of England can never think of consenting to a war against Holland unless he have in his prospect sufficient supplies to set out his whole naval force and to maintain it during the war; and consequently it must be an opinion very erroneously grounded that thirty or forty English ships joining with the French fleet can be sufficient to prosecute the war with advantage and security to England....

... On the other side, if the King of England set out his whole fleet and be out before the Dutch all the forementioned advantages will accrue to England by destroying and interrupting their whole trade, taking their ships and blocking up their harbours, in a word totally disabling their Government, if the country be at the same time vigorously attacked by land while we are in a state of this pressing and molesting them by sea.

CHARLES II AND MADAME
by C. H. Hartmann   Heinemann, 1934   *pp.292–295*

(This memorandum is in the hand of Sir Thomas Clifford, who was in charge of the negotiations with France, but it represents Charles's views.)

The Secret Treaty of Dover (1670) (the official Whig version):

Colbert de Croissy, Ambassador from France to the Court of England, after having set forth to the King of England all the reasons he had to be dissatisfied with the Dutch, after reminding him of the medals in which the Dutch attributed to themselves all the honour of the Peace of Aix-la-Chapelle and treated the mediation of England with so much contempt, he at last gave him to know that the time was come of being revenged upon a nation that had so little respect for Kings, and he could never meet with a more favourable opportunity. Upon this representation that Prince sign'd a private treaty with France; and, to give him farther assurances upon the matter, Henrietta of England, Duchess of Orleans, a Princess whose wit and capacity was equal to her beauty, sister to the King of England and sister-in-law to the King of France, cross'd over to England in 1670, and in the name of the

Most Christian King made a proposal to her royal brother of ensuring to him an absolute authority over his Parliament re-establishing the Catholic religion in the three kingdoms of England, Scotland and Ireland. But with the same breath she gave him to know that there was a necessity above all things of lowering the pride and power of the Dutch, and of reducing that State to the narrow compass of the Province of Holland, of which the Prince of Orange should be Sovereign, or, at least, perpetual Stadholder; that by this scheme the King of England should have Zealand for a retreat in case of necessity, and the rest of the Netherlands should remain in the hands of the King of France if he could make himself master of it.

STATE TRACTS, 1682, vol. 1   p.10

The Secret Treaty of Dover (the secret clause):

The King of Great Britain, being convinced of the truth of the Catholic religion, and resolved to make his declaration of it and to be reconciled to the Church of Rome, as soon as the good of his kingdom's affairs shall permit him, . . . thinks that the best means to prevent [public] tranquillity being checked is to be assured in case of need of the assistance of his most Christian Majesty, who promises to furnish to the King of Great Britain . . . the sum of 2,000,000 livres tournoises . . . and, further, that the said King obliges himself to assist his Britannic Majesty as often as there shall be need, to the number of 6,000 men; . . . the day for the said declaration of Catholicism shall be entirely in the option of the King of Great Britain.

Translated from the French in HISTORY OF ENGLAND, vol. 11
by J. Lingard London, 1837   pp.367–368

Declaration of Indulgence for Tender Consciences, 15 March 1672:

And in the first place, we declare our express resolution, meaning and intention to be, that the Church of England be preserved, and remain entire in its doctrine, discipline, and government, as now it stands established by law; and that this be taken to be, as it is, the basis, rule and standard, of the general and public worship of God, and that the orthodox conformable clergy do receive and enjoy the revenues belonging thereunto; and that no person, though of a different opinion and persuasion, shall be exempt from paying his tithes or other dues whatsoever. And further, we declare, that no person shall be capable of holding any benefice, living, or ecclesiastical dignity or preferment of any kind in this our kingdom of England, who is not exactly conformable.

We do in the next place declare our will and pleasure to be, that the execution of all and all manner of penal laws in matters ecclesiastical, against whatsoever sort of Nonconformists or recusants, be immediately suspended. And all judges, judges of assize and gaol-delivery, sheriffs, justices of the peace, mayors, bailiffs, and other officers whatsoever, whether ecclesiastical or civil, are to take notice of it, and pay due obedience thereunto.

And that there may be no pretence for any of our subjects to continue their illegal meetings and conventicles, we do declare, that we shall from time to time allow a sufficient number of places, as they shall be desired, in all parts of this our kingdom, for the use of such as do not conform to the Church of England, to meet and assemble in order to their public worship and devotion, which places shall be open and free to all persons.

But to prevent such disorders and inconveniencies as may happen by this our indulgence, if not duly regulated, and that they may be the better protected by the civil magistrate, our express will and pleasure is, that none of our subjects do presume to meet in any place, until such place be allowed, and the teacher of that congregation be approved by us.

And lest any should apprehend, that this restriction should make our said allowance and approbation difficult to be obtained, we do further declare, that this our indulgence, as to the allowance of the public places of worship, and approbation of the teachers, shall extend to all sorts of Nonconformists and recusants, except the recusants of the Roman Catholic religion, to whom we shall in no wise allow public places of worship, but only indulge them their share in the common exemption from the execution of the penal laws, and the exercise of their worship in their private houses only.

DOCUMENTARY ANNALS OF THE REFORMED CHURCH OF ENGLAND, vol. 2
by E. Cardwell   O.U.P., 1844   *pp.334–336*

Speech by Charles to both Houses of Parliament, 8 March 1673:

My Lords and Gentlemen: Yesterday you presented me an Address, as the best means for the satisfying and composing the minds of my subjects; to which I freely and readily agreed. And I shall take care to see it performed accordingly.

I hope, on the other side, you, gentlemen of the House of Commons, will do your part; for I must put you in mind it is near five weeks since I demanded a supply; and what you voted unanimously upon it, did both give life to my affairs at home, and disheartened my enemies abroad. But the seeming delay it hath met withal since, hath made them take new courage; and they are now preparing for this next summer a greater fleet (as they say) than ever they had yet; so that, if the supply be not very speedily dispatched, it will be altogether ineffectual; and the safety, honour, and interest of England must of necessity be exposed. Pray lay this to your heart; and let not the fears and jealousies of some draw an inevitable ruin upon us all.

Louis XIV and Charles II

> My Lords and Gentlemen: If there be any scruple remain with you concerning the suspension of penal laws, I here faithfully promise you that what hath been done in that particular shall not for the future be drawn either into consequence or example. And as I daily expect from you a Bill for my supply, so, I assure you, I shall as willingly receive and pass any other you shall offer me, that may tend to the giving you satisfaction in all your just grievances.
>
> JOURNALS OF THE HOUSE OF LORDS, 1666–1675   p.549

Finally, three historians debate the motives and effectiveness of Charles's French policy.

G. M. D. Howat:
> Protestant and Catholic alike toiled to make possible the ambitions of the king. 'It would be easy to find tyrants more odious than Louis XIV; but there was not one who ever used his power to inflict greater suffering or wrong.' Such was the harsh judgement of the nineteenth-century Catholic historian Lord Acton.
>
> This was the king who was to dominate Europe for a further thirty years after Charles II's death. This was the king to whom Charles II was linked by treaty, financial need, a hint of blackmail and a common acceptance of absolutism in princes.
>
> STUART AND CROMWELLIAN FOREIGN POLICY
> *by G. M. D. Howat   A & C Black, 1974*   p.148

Sir Keith Feiling:
> He had, no doubt, an admiration of the French monarchy, and a correspondingly hearty distrust of the House of Commons, whose interference, among other things, he judged had been fatal to his father's foreign affairs. . . . But the Navy and our sea-power were his real political passion. He was incessantly jealous of the Dutch fleet, and his happiest relaxations, until Newmarket claimed him, were inspecting the dockyards at Chatham, or discussing naval design with Pepys and Pett. For the Navy alone he was ready to make personal sacrifice, and in 1677 paid largely from his Privy Purse to complete the ships for which parliamentary grants had, as predicted, proved inadequate. . . . His assets, considered as of the old diplomatic school, were considerable. He was a master of dissimulation, indeed of falsehood; calculated indiscretion was a weapon in which he excelled; he knew the inside of a Frenchman's mind. Nor must the love of ease justly attributed to him overshadow his ceaseless activity in business.
>
> BRITISH FOREIGN POLICY, 1660–1672
> *by Sir Keith Feiling   Macmillan, 1930*   pp.24–26

John Miller:
> I find it hard to believe that Charles seriously intended to declare himself a Catholic, as he must have been well aware of what the

reaction of his Protestant subjects would have been. If he did not intend to turn Catholic, there were several reasons why he might have said that he intended to do so: in order to get money, or to control the timing of the war, or to force secretary Arlington to accept an alliance of which he disapproved or to give Louis XIV an added inducement to conclude a personal union. Of these four possible reasons only the last is satisfactory. I am inclined to reject the first two for the reasons given below and the third is, I think, over-subtle and has little evidence to back it up. On the other hand it is quite plausible that 'Catholicity' should have been an extra bait for Louis XIV which Charles hastily dropped once the alliance had been secured. Then he and Louis concentrated on what was for both of them the main concern, the Dutch war.

POPERY AND POLITICS IN ENGLAND, 1660–1688
by John Miller   C.U.P., 1973   *pp.110–111*

3 Politics 1678-1681

How did the Exclusion Crisis arise, and how did Charles II survive it?

Background to the crisis

'Things have come to a pretty pass', a nineteenth-century politician once remarked, without evident self-parody, 'if religion should be allowed to interfere in our daily lives.' During the Civil War and Interregnum, religious enthusiasts had a wonderful time, but after the Restoration, politics became less bound up with religion. The history of Restoration politics, however, is only just beginning to recover from the pieties of the Whig interpretation and to be treated as a subject in its own right. Much more research still needs to be done, but recent writing has modified the traditional view that it was Charles who spoiled the relationship with his Parliaments. The root of his conflict with Parliament lay in the grant, inadequate in amount and inefficiently collected, which was made to him at the beginning of his reign. This situation forced Charles to accept secret, though small and irregular, payments from his cousin, Louis XIV. After the partial bankruptcy of the Crown in 1672, developments in English trade and the capture of markets from the Dutch gave Charles financial independence of Parliament – as long as he kept his country out of war thereafter. In fact Parliament did not know that Louis could virtually blackmail Charles into keeping out of war with him by threatening to reveal the clause in the Secret Treaty of Dover in which Charles promised to become a Catholic. Moreover, Charles's equivocal attitude to Parliament did not help matters, as the extracts printed below indicate.

Charles II's speech on opening Parliament, 15 February 1677:

> I declare myself very plainly to you that I come prepared to give you all the satisfaction and security in the great concerns of the Protestant religion, as it is established in the Church of England, that shall reasonably be asked, or can consist with Christian prudence. And I declare myself as freely, that I am ready to gratify you in a further securing of your liberty and property (if you can

> think you want it) by as many good laws as you shall propose, and as can consist with the safety of the government; without which, there will neither be liberty nor property left to any man.
> JOURNALS OF THE HOUSE OF LORDS, 1675–1681   p.36

Letter of Charles II to Lord Chancellor Finch, 24 July 1678:
> I do find by what my Lord Yarmouth hath showed me, that the commission is not yet gone forth for the Justices of peace in Norfolk, therefore I see no inconvenience in leaving Sir J. Hobart, Sir J. Holland and Sir R. Kempe out of the peace, at least the two first. For there is no objection against it but in disobliging those sort of people who will never be obliged, and any countenance I give them is only used against myself and Government.
> *Historical Manuscripts Commission; Finch MSS, vol. 2*   p.42

The Popish Plot

In the prevailing atmosphere of hysteria against the French and the Catholics, most people believed Titus Oates's allegations of a Catholic plot to murder the King and replace him by James. But reactions differed, as the extracts show. They also show the extent to which Charles was prepared to follow Danby's plan to use the wave of relief at the news of the King's safe delivery from the 'plot' to carry him to the front of a popular nationalist movement.

An anonymous account of the plot:
> Doctor Stillingfleet having been attempted by a fellow in a gentile habit, who brought a counterfeit letter as from the bishop of London to desire him to come to him in the evening, and brought a coach to carry him, intending to have served him as Sir Edmund Godfrey was, but was prevented; partly an extraordinary business would not permit him to go out, and partly jealousy, which made the doctor answer him if he could go he would make use of his own coach, which made the fellow vanish, and the doctor, waiting on the bishop the next day, found the letter and pretence wholly counterfeit. Thereupon on Sunday about forty persons a guard waited on the doctor to church and home.
> ENGLISH HISTORICAL DOCUMENTS, vol. 8 (1660–1714)
> *edited by A. Browning   Eyre & Spottiswoode, 1953*   p.112

John Dryden:
> From hence began that Plot, the nation's curse,
> Bad in itself, but represented worse,
> Raised in extremes, and in extremes decried,
> With oaths affirmed, with dying vows denied,
> Not weighed or winnowed by the multitude,
> But swallowed in the mass, unchewed and crude.

Thomas Osborne, Earl of Danby

> Some truth there was, but dashed and brewed with lies
> To please the fools and puzzle all the wise.
> Succeeding times did equal folly call
> Believing nothing or believing all.
>
> *From Absalom and Achitophel*
> quoted in THE WORKS OF JOHN DRYDEN, vol. I
> edited by James Kinsley   O.U.P., 1958   *pp.219–220*

Letter of Lady Fox to her daughter, 30 October 1678:
> Here is great strictness in Whitehall; all the locks changed of the privy lodgings and all the gates of the courts kept shut and none suffered to come in but who are known. The French cook and the confectionary are discharged already by the King's command and

there is no other Papist below stairs, but when it comes to the remove above stairs I doubt it will not be so easily done. I am heartily sorry for our good friends who must suffer with the rest if this be pursued, as I believe it will; for it is most certain that the House of Commons will do no manner of thing till all this be effectually done.

ESSEX RECORD OFFICE D/DBy C14; Audley End Archives

Speech of Charles to Parliament, 21 October 1678:

I now intend to acquaint you (as I shall always do with anything that concerns me), that I have been informed of a design against my person by the Jesuits; of which I shall forbear any opinion, lest I may seem to say too much, or too little. But I will leave the matter to the law; and, in the meantime, will take as much care as I can to prevent all manners of practices by that sort of men, and of others too, who have been tampering in a high degree by foreigners, and contriving how to introduce Popery amongst us.

JOURNALS OF THE HOUSE OF LORDS, 1675–1681   p.293

Letter of Charles to the Marquess of Ormonde (Lord Lieutenant of Ireland, and a Cavalier), 5 November 1678:

You may easily believe that I have not a little business now upon my hands. This bearer will inform you so particularly of all as I need not tell you my opinion of it nor enter farther upon the matter. I am sure you will put things into the best posture where you are, that may be upon all events so as I shall say no more to you, only to assure you that I have that confidence in you and kindness for you, as you may be assured of my constant friendship.

Historical Manuscripts Commission; Ormonde MSS, vol. 14, Part 7 p.25

The crisis

It is arguable that the crisis was avoidable and that a genuine national settlement, based on Protestantism at home and abroad, might have been made, had it not foundered on the cliffs of the Treaty of Dover. On the other hand, although people spoke nostalgically of Cromwell's Protestant crusading foreign policy, the time had passed when such was practical or even necessary. Granted Parliament's mistrust and Charles's absence of freedom, all the major events preceding the crisis do seem to lead up to it: Clarendon's fall, the dissolution of the Cabal (the name given to Charles's informal body of five advisers: Clifford, Arlington, Buckingham, Ashley and Lauderdale), and the impeachment of Danby. Attempting to save Danby, Charles dissolved Parliament, but the new Parliament was more mistrustful than ever, and Charles had to concede Danby's resignation. This, with the Popish Plot and the organization of the opposition under Shaftesbury, led to the first Bill to exclude the Catholic Duke of York from the succession to the throne.

It is possible to disagree, also, about the nature of the crisis, because points of view depend on how Charles and the opposition are assessed. The evidence is in conflict, for example, on the extent to which the Whigs were a real party, better organized than their opponents. Dryden and Burnet have the disadvantages of people who write subsequently about events that happened in their own lifetimes; Barillon shows how complex was the situation; Monmouth, Shaftesbury's protégé, throws light on his own character and on the nature of his claim to the throne; and the language of the Exclusion Bill itself repays careful study.

Professor Andrew Browning on Dr J. R. Jones:

> Fashions change in the historical world no less than elsewhere, and the word 'party', so long under a cloud, seems now to be experiencing some measure of rehabilitation. In *The First Whigs. The Politics of the Exclusion Crisis, 1678–1683* (London: O.U.P. for the University of Durham, 1961, 30s.), Dr. J. R. Jones argues persuasively in favour of the recognition of the Exclusion Whigs as a genuine party, basing his case on an exhaustive examination of the elections to the three Exclusion parliaments, the tactics pursued in these parliaments and the political literature of the time. Possibly he exaggerates the strength of the organization, which was of short duration and suffered a catastrophic collapse; but it is unlikely that his main contention will be seriously challenged or that the value of the material he has unearthed will fail of recognition. Inevitably, however, he has associated his account of the party with an assessment of the character and aims of its creator and leader, and on that highly controversial matter there is not likely to be the same unanimity. Few politicians of the first rank have made as many outrageous and almost inexplicable blunders as the first earl of Shaftesbury. His countenancing of the treaty of Dover policy and more particularly his *Delenda est Carthago* speech, his issue of writs for the election of members of parliament without authority from the Speaker, his attempt to maintain that parliament was dissolved by the long prorogation of 1675 and his extravagant support of Titus Oates were all errors against which much less astute men might easily have warned him, as indeed some did. The explanation generally offered of these and similar aberrations on his part is that he had few if any principles to restrain him from embarking on any course that happened to catch his fancy and a confidence in his own cleverness which made him believe he could extricate himself unharmed from any dilemma in which he might be landed. But Dr. Jones refuses to see in Shaftesbury a mere clever adventurer and makes a good case for his views. His picture of the Whig leader is indeed such as one would like to accept, not excessively favourable, consistent in itself

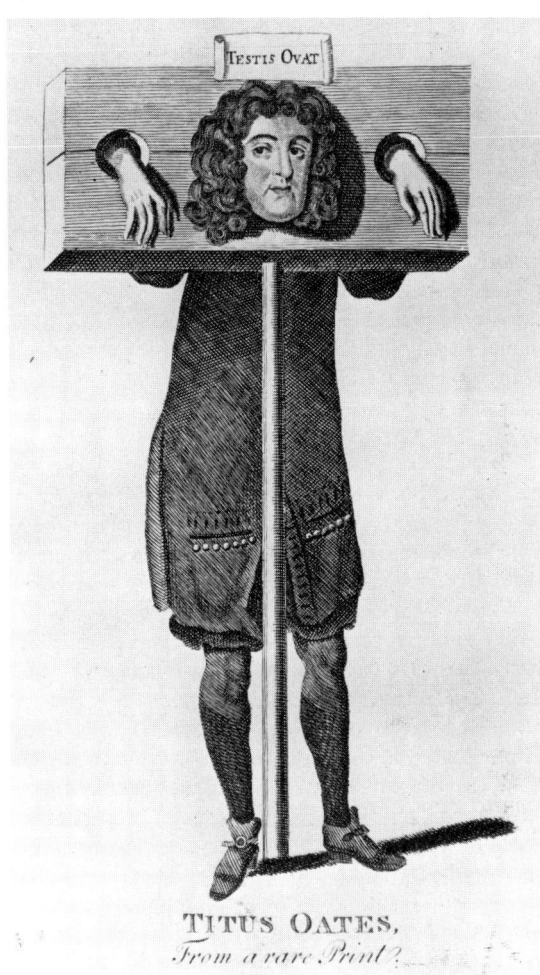

Titus Oates, inventor of the 'Popish Plot'

and also with Shaftesbury's activities in the short period of which this volume treats, suggestive of a man partially tamed, as Shaftesbury may well have been, by advancing years and a premonition of impending disaster. The difficulty remains, however, of reconciling it with so much that went before, and the task of meeting this difficulty is one which Dr. Jones, not unreasonably in view of the restricted character of his main subject, does not attempt.

Gilbert Burnet:
> ... a great party was formed, who declared more heartily for the Protestant religion and for the interest of England ... the Earl of Shaftesbury opened many of their eyes, and let them know the designs of the court; and indeed they were then so visible that there were enough seen without such secret intelligence to convince the most incredulous. Sir William Coventry ... Colonel Birch ... Waller ... the Lord Russell and the Lord Cavendish ... Littleton and Powle ... Sir Thomas Lee ... These were the chief men that preserved the nation from a deceitful and practising court, and from a corrupt House of Commons; and by their skill and firmness they, from a small number who began the opposition, grew at last to be the majority.
>
> HISTORY OF MY OWN TIME, vol. 2
> *edited by O. Airy   O.U.P., 1897–1900*   pp.89–93

Report by Paul Barillon to Louis XIV, 1679 (Barillon appended to this report a list of Members, both Whig and Tory, who had accepted pensions and presents. Lord Holles, the example given below, was one of the more scrupulous of the recipients.):

> Conformable to the orders your Majesty has given me, I have re-entered into a correspondence with the persons in Parliament who I thought might be useful to your service hereafter. I had always kept measures with them to make use of them in time of need. I shall at present give your Majesty the detail, as you order by your last dispatch.
>
> I have at all times taken great care to manage Lord Holles, and I believe I have kept him in very favourable sentiments for your Majesty's interests. He is the man of all England for whom the different cabals have the most consideration. He is respected in general by all parties, but principally by the Presbyterians. Nothing did me so much service with him as the offer I made him on your Majesty's part of a box with your picture set with diamonds. He made great acknowledgments for this mark of your Majesty's esteem; but he has not accepted the present, and I have it still. I have pressed him many times to take it. He has always excused himself, and told me that he should serve your Majesty with less scruple and more usefully if he did not accept it, and that he could not resolve to take it without the permission of the king of Great Britain, being at present of his Council. I opposed with very good reasons the proposal he made to me of telling his Britannic Majesty that your Majesty would make him a present.
>
> *From Sir John Dalrymple: Memoirs*
> quoted in ENGLISH HISTORICAL DOCUMENTS, vol. 8 (1660–1714)
> *edited by A. Browning   Eyre & Spottiswoode, 1953*   p.251

Dryden on Shaftesbury:
> For Close Designs, and crooked Counsels fit:
> Sagacious, Bold, and Turbulent of wit:
> Restless, unfixt in Principles and Place;
> In Pow'r unpleased impatient of Disgrace.
> In fiery Soul, which working out its way,
> Fretted the Pigmy Body to decay:
> And o'r informed the Tenement of Clay.
> A daring Pilot in extremity;
> Pleased with the Danger, when the Waves went high
> He sought the Storms; but for a Calm unfit,
> Would Steer too nigh the Sands, to boast his Wit.
> Great Wits are sure to Madness near allied;
> And thin Partitions do their Bounds divide:
> Else, why should he, with Wealth and Honour blest,
> Refuse his Age the needful hours of Rest?
> Punish a Body which he could not please;
> Bankrupt of Life, yet Prodigal of Ease?

From Absalom and Achitophel, quoted in THE WORKS OF JOHN DRYDEN, vol. I
edited by James Kinsley   O.U.P., 1958   *pp.219–220*

A miniature by Cooper: James, Duke of York

The Exclusion Bill:
> Whereas James, duke of York, is notoriously known to have been perverted from the Protestant to the popish religion, whereby not

only great encouragement hath been given to the popish party to enter into and carry on most devilish and horrid plots and conspiracies for the destruction of his Majesty's sacred person and government, and for the extirpation of the true Protestant religion, but also, if the said duke should succeed to the imperial crown of this realm, nothing is more manifest than that a total change of religion within these kingdoms would ensue, for the prevention whereof be it therefore enacted ... that the said James, duke of York, shall be and is by authority of this present Parliament excluded and made for ever incapable to inherit, possess or enjoy the imperial crown of this realm and of the kingdom of Ireland and the dominions and territories to them or either of them belonging, or to have, exercise or enjoy any dominion, power, jurisdiction or authority within the same kingdoms, dominions or any of them.

From Manuscripts of the House of Lords, 1678–1688, pp.195–197 quoted in ENGLISH HISTORICAL DOCUMENTS, vol. 8 (1660–1714) *edited by A. Browning   Eyre & Spottiswoode, 1953*   *p.119*

Declaration of the Duke of Monmouth on claiming the title of King (Although the Declaration was made in 1685, it adequately represents the attitudes of Monmouth, Shaftesbury and their followers in 1679–1681.):

Whereas upon our first landing at Lyme in the County of Dorset on Thursday the 11th day of this instant month of June, we did publish a declaration in the name of ourself, by the name of James, duke of Monmouth, and the noblemen, gentlemen and others now in arms for defence and vindication of the Protestant religion, and of the laws, rights and privileges of England, from the invasion made upon them, and for delivering the kingdom from the usurpation and tyranny of James, duke of York; wherein amongst other things therein contained we did declare that out of the love we bear to the English nation, whose welfare and settlement we did infinitely prefer to whatever might concern ourselves, we would not at present insist upon our title, but leave the determination thereof to the authority of a Parliament legally chosen and acting with freedom; since which it hath pleased Almighty God to succeed and prosper us hitherto in a very eminent manner, and also disposed the hearts of our loving subjects that from all parts of the country they flock in unanimously for the defence of our person and of the righteous cause we are engaged in; by which we have been enabled to march from Lyme aforesaid unto our good town of Taunton to the terror and amazement of all our enemies round about us: and whereas as well during our said march as since our coming to Taunton aforesaid all our loving subjects have with warm and repeated solicitations importuned us to exert and take upon us our sovereign and royal authority of king as well as of the power of a general, that we might thereby be enabled to make use of the laws and statutes of the realm in conjunction with our arms for their safety and preservation; and have likewise earnestly implored us for their own sakes not to defer the execution of our kingly office to so late a period as is mentioned in the said declaration, for that it will in all probability render the progress of our arms more slow, and thereby give our enemies a longer season to harass and impoverish our kingdom: we could not but with great reluctancy incline to consent to anything that might seem to be a departure from our said declaration, and thereby raise any diffidence amongst the sober and virtuous, or give occasion to wicked and malicious men to arraign the sincerity of our intentions; but as the said clause in the said declaration was inserted under this prospect, to convince the world that we postponed all things to the safety and welfare of our people, and that we consulted not so much our own interest as their prosperity, being so convinced both from the circumstances of affairs and from united advice of all our loving people's petitions that it was absolutely necessary for their protection and defence that we should immediately insist upon our title to the crowns of England, Scotland, France and Ireland, and the dominions and territories thereunto belonging, as son and heir apparent to Charles the Second, king of England, our royal father lately deceased: we have therefore suffered ourselves to be prevailed upon, and have complied with the earnest importunities and necessities of our people, giving way to our being proclaimed king on the 20th day of this instant June at our town of Taunton aforesaid.

Historical Manuscripts Commission; Bath MSS, vol. 2   *pp.170–171*

The end of the crisis

Historians, like the gods, love a winner. But the impartial judge of history, in order to be fair to both sides, must remember that the opposition came close to winning. In hindsight, Charles's habitual inactivity may have received the epithet 'masterly' merely because he won. A study of the evidence reveals the one principle on which he was immovable and some of the tactics (for he had no strategy) which he used. Readers must decide how much credit to give to Halifax and what factors saved him from impeachment. Finally, James and Charles, the latter appealing for vindication directly to his people, give two versions of how exclusion was defeated. The discovery of the Rye House Plot seems like an anticlimax.

Burnet on the passing of Habeas Corpus:
> The former parliament had passed a very strict act for the due execution of the habeas corpus, which was indeed all they did. It

was carried by an odd artifice in the house of lords. Lord Grey and lord Norris were named to be the tellers. Lord Norris, being a man subject to vapours, was not at all times attentive to what he was doing: so a very fat lord coming in, lord Grey counted him for ten, as a jest at first, but seeing lord Norris had not observed that, he went on with his misreckoning of ten for one: so it was reported to the house, and declared that they who were for the bill were the majority, though it indeed went on the other side: and by this means the bill passed.

HISTORY OF MY OWN TIME, vol. 2
edited by O. Airy   O.U.P., 1897–1900   *pp.263–264*

(This story agrees with a discrepancy between the number of lords that day in the House and those counted in the division, as recorded in the House's Minute Book.)

Speeches of Charles to Parliament, 9 November 1678:

I am as ready to join with you in all the ways and means that may establish a firm security of the Protestant religion as your own hearts can wish. And this not only during my time, of which I am sure you have no fear, but in future ages, even to the end of the world.

And therefore I am come to assure you that whatsoever Bills you shall present, to be passed into laws, to make you safe in the reign of my successor (so they tend not to impeach the right of succession, nor the descent of the Crown in the true line; and so as they restrain not my power, nor the just rights of any Protestant successor) shall find from me a ready concurrence.

And I desire you withal, to think of some more effectual means for the conviction of Popish recusants, and to expedite your councils as fast as you can, that the world may see our unanimity; and that I may have an opportunity of showing you how ready I am to do anything that may give comfort and satisfaction to such dutiful and loyal subjects.

JOURNALS OF THE HOUSE OF LORDS, 1675–1681   *p.345*

30 December 1678:

My Lords and Gentlemen: It is with great unwillingness that I come this day to tell you, I intend to prorogue you. I think all of you are witnesses that I have been ill used; the particulars of it I intend to acquaint you with at a more convenient time. In the meantime, I do assure you that I will immediately enter upon the disbanding of the Army, and let all the world see that there is nothing that I intend but for the good of the kingdom, and for the safety of religion. I will likewise prosecute this plot, and find out who are the instruments in it: and I shall take all the care which lies in my power, for the security of religion, and the maintenance of it

BABEL and BETHEL: or, The POPE in his Colours.

WITH

The Church of ENGLAND's Supplication to his Majesty, our gracious Soveraign, the true Defender of the Faith; To protect her from all the Machinations of Rome, and its bloody Emissaries.

An Anti-Catholic broadsheet

as it is now established. I have no more to say to you at this time, but leave the rest to my Lord Chancellor to prorogue you.
JOURNALS OF THE HOUSE OF LORDS, 1675–1681 p.447

6 March 1679:

My Lords and Gentlemen: I meet you here with the most earnest desire that man can have to unite the minds of all my subjects, both to me, and to one another. And I resolve it shall be your faults, if the success be not suitably to my desires. I have done many great things already in order to that end; as, the exclusion of the Popish Lords from their seats in Parliament; the execution of several men, both upon the score of the Plot and of the murder of Sir Edmund Berry Godfrey. And it is apparent that I have not been idle in prosecuting the discovery of both, as much further as hath been possible in so short a time.

I have disbanded as much of the Army as I could get money to do; and I am ready to disband the rest, so soon as you shall reimburse what they have cost me, and will enable me to pay off the remainder. And, above all, I have commanded my brother to absent himself from me, because I would not leave the most malicious man room to say I had not removed all causes which could be pretended to influence me towards Popish Counsels.
JOURNALS OF THE HOUSE OF LORDS, 1675–1681 p.450

Burnet on Halifax:

He was a man of a great and ready wit, full of life, and very pleasant, much turned to satire. He let his wit run much on matters of religion, so that he passed for a bold and determined atheist; though he often protested to me he was not one; and said he believed there was not one in the world. He confessed he could not swallow down every thing that divines imposed on the world. He was a Christian in submission, and he believed as much as he could, and he hoped God would not lay it to his charge if he could not digest iron, as an ostrich did, nor take into his belief things that must burst him: if he had any scruples, they were not sought for, nor cherished by him; for he never read an atheistical book. These were his excuses, but I could not quite believe him; yet in a fit of sickness I knew him very much touched with a sense of religion. I was then oft with him: he seemed full of good purposes: but they went off with his sickness. He was always talking of morality and friendship. He was punctual in all payments, and just in all his private dealings; but with relation to the public he went backwards and forwards, and changed sides so often, that in conclusion no side trusted him. He seemed full of commonwealth notions, yet he went in to the worst part of king Charles's reign. He was out of measure vain and ambitious. The liveliness of his imagination was

> always too hard for his judgment. A severe jest was preferred by him to all arguments whatsoever; and he was endless in consultations. For when after much discourse a point was settled, if he could find a new jest to make even that which was suggested by himself seem ridiculous, he could not hold, but would study to raise the credit of his wit, though it made others call his judgment in question. When he talked to me as a philosopher of his contempt of the world, I asked him what he meant, to be getting so many new titles, which I called the hanging himself about with bells and tinsel. He had no other excuse for it but this, that, since the world were such fools as to value those matters, a man must be a fool for company: he considered them but as rattles: yet rattles please children: so these might be of use to his family.
>
> HISTORY OF MY OWN TIME, vol. I
> *edited by O. Airy   O.U.P., 1897–1900*   *pp.484–485*

(Burnet disliked Halifax's sense of humour, which was sometimes used at the Bishop's expense.)

Speech on impeachment attributed to the Earl of Carnarvon (This speech was made in 1678, and it applies to Danby, but it can apply to the situation faced by Halifax.):

> My Lords, I understand but little of Latin, but a good deal of English, and not a little of the English history, from which I have learnt the mischiefs of such kind of prosecutions as these, and the ill fate of the prosecutors. I could bring many instances, and those very ancient; but, my Lords, I shall go no farther back than the latter end of Queen Elizabeth's reign, at which time the earl of Essex was run down by Sir Walter Ralegh. My Lord Bacon, he ran down Sir Walter Ralegh, and your Lordships know what became of my Lord Bacon. The duke of Buckingham, he ran down my Lord Bacon, and your Lordships know what happened to the duke of Buckingham. Sir Thomas Wentworth, afterwards earl of Strafford, ran down the duke of Buckingham, and you all know what became of him. Sir Harry Vane, he ran down the earl of Strafford, and your Lordships know what became of Sir Harry Vane. Chancellor Hyde, he ran down Sir Harry Vane, and your Lordships know what became of the Chancellor. Sir Thomas Osborne, now earl of Danby, ran down Chancellor Hyde, but what will become of the earl of Danby your Lordships best can tell. But let me see that man that dare run the earl of Danby down, and we shall soon see what will become of him.
>
> ENGLISH HISTORICAL DOCUMENTS, vol. 8 (1660–1714)
> *edited by A. Browning   Eyre & Spottiswoode, 1953*   *pp.203–204*

The King's reply to an address by the Commons for the removal of the Marquess of Halifax, 1680:

CHARLES R.

His Majesty, having received the address of this House relating to the earl of Halifax, hath thought fit to return this answer:

That he conceives the said address to be liable to several exceptions; but, having a great desire to preserve all possible good understanding with this House, he chooses to decline to enter into particulars, to avoid all occasions of dispute. He therefore thinks fit to tell them that he doth not find the grounds in the address of this House to be sufficient to induce him to remove the earl of Halifax; but he answers them at the same time that whenever this House shall, in a due and regular course, prove any crime either against the said earl of Halifax or any other person, who either now is or shall hereafter be in his Council, he will leave him or them to their own legal defence without interposing to protect them.

JOURNALS OF THE HOUSE OF COMMONS, vol. 9   *p.663*

Royal declaration to be read in all churches, 1681:

We opened the last Parliament, which was held at Westminster, with as gracious expressions of our readiness to satisfy the desires of our good subjects and to secure them against all their just fears, as the weighty consideration either of preserving the Established Religion and the liberty and property of our subjects at home, or of supporting our neighbours and allies abroad, could fill our heart with, or possibly require from us. And we do solemnly declare, that we did intend, as far as would have consisted with the very being of the Government, to have complied with anything that could have been proposed to us to accomplish those ends. We asked of them the supporting the alliances we had made for the preservation of the general peace in Christendom. We recommended to them the further examination of the Plot. We desired their advice and assistance concerning the preservation of Tangier. We offered to concur in any remedies that could be proposed for the security of the Protestant religion, that might consist with preserving the succession of the Crown in its due and legal course of descent. To all which we met with most unsuitable returns from the House of Commons: – addresses, in the nature of remonstrances rather than of answers; arbitrary orders for taking our subjects into custody for matters that had no relation to privileges of Parliament; strange illegal votes, declaring divers eminent persons to be enemies to the King and kingdom, without any order or process of law, any hearing of their defence, or any proof so much as offered against them. . . .

Which we had no sooner dissolved but we caused another to be assembled at Oxford; at the opening of which we thought it necessary to give them warning of the errors of the former, in hopes to have prevented the like miscarriages. And we required of them to make the laws of the land their rule; as we did, and do resolve, they shall be ours. We further added, that what we had formerly and so often declared concerning the succession we would not depart from; but to remove all reasonable fears that might arise from the possibility of a Popish successor's coming to the Crown, if means could be found that in such a case the administration of the Government might remain in Protestant hands, we were ready to hearken to any expedient by which the religion established might be preserved, and the monarchy not destroyed. But contrary to our offers and expectation, we saw that no expedient would be entertained but that of a total exclusion, which we had so often declared was a point that in our own royal judgement so nearly concerned us both in honour, justice and conscience that we could never consent to it. . . .

But notwithstanding all this, let not the restless malice of ill men who are labouring to poison our people, some out of fondness for their old beloved Commonwealth principles, and some out of anger at their being disappointed in the particular designs they had for the accomplishment of their own ambition and greatness, persuade any of our good subjects that we intend to lay aside the use of Parliaments.

From History of England, vol. 3 by L. Eachard
quoted in LETTERS, SPEECHES AND DECLARATIONS OF KING CHARLES II
edited by Sir A. Bryant   Cassell, 1935   *pp.320–321*

The Duke of York on the crisis:

January 1681. The Parliament impeach the Duke of York's friends. The King prorogues them; but they first passed some violent votes. One to meet at Oxford on the twenty-first of March .... The King, to prepare for the Oxford Parliament, had some guards with him; and quartered the best part of Oxford's regiment on the road to secure his return. He left a body to secure the city. . . . 22 February. The House of Commons, not better composed than the last, resolved, at some of their cabals, to begin with the Bill of Exclusion. . . . 28 March. The House of Commons, being enraged, ordered in the Bill of Exclusion on Saturday night. It was read the first time on Monday, and ordered a second reading, when the King sent for them to the House of Lords; and, to their great surprise, appeared in his robes. The Lords, ignorant of it, had not theirs. He dissolved them, took coach immediately, and went that night to Windsor. This struck them, like thunder, with amazement. It gave the King great reputation. His friends took courage. The faction were in the greatest rage and despair. The King still would not let the Duke of York return till he saw how matters went; and till he had reformed the lieutenancy of the

> city, the justices of the peace, and the militia throughout the kingdom.
>
> *From James II: Memoirs*
> *quoted in* ORIGINAL PAPERS, VOL. I
> *by J. Macpherson   Strahan and Cadell, 1775*   *pp.113–117*

The Rye House Plot (the Duke of Ormonde to the Earl of Arran, 22 June 1683):

> The king has appointed a Council to be held at Hampton Court tomorrow in the morning, and will hold another in the afternoon. The principal occasion is the discovery of a damnable conspiracy for killing the king and the duke as they came from Newmarket to London this last spring; and, though I am as slow as any man in my belief of such discoveries and attempts, yet I believe it highly probable that the thing would have been attempted, if the fire which burned a great part of Newmarket had not driven the king from thence eight or ten days sooner than he intended and prefixed for his stay there. The discoverer is a substantial citizen, zealously factious and active on the Whig party, and so bold that it was he that arrested the lord mayor when nobody else could be found hardy enough to undertake it. He says it was remorse of conscience and horror of so bloody a fact, and for prevention of the like villainy, that moved him to repent and discover, and we are charitably to believe him, though the fear of some of the conspirators being beforehand with him might have some share in his conversion.
>
> *Historical Manuscripts Commission; Ormonde MSS N.S., vol. 8*
>
> *pp.51–52*

Religion

4

What were the aims of Charles's religious policy?

Introduction

Historians disagree about the true nature of the King's religious convictions – or whether he had any at all. His pious remarks on receiving copies of the Bible, or the attentiveness with which he read a tract by Father John Hudleston's uncle while hiding at Moseley from Cromwell's soldiers, may have been merely a polite way of thanking his benefactors. The motives behind his religious policy of toleration are difficult to fathom. Why did he not join in the general outcry against Nonconformists at the time of the Restoration, when it might have seemed politically expedient to do so? There is no evidence that he believed in toleration as an abstract principle, or that he had any appreciation of Puritan or Quaker spirituality. It is instructive to note the differences between Charles's stated wishes and the laws imposed by Parliament between 1661 and 1665, defining the position of the Church of England and imposing disabilities on those who failed to conform. Was Charles's Declaration of Indulgence (see Chapter Two) a reaction to Parliament's opposition; a political move to appease the storm of protest which had greeted a harsher form of the Conventicle Act (1670); or the first step in his conversion to Catholicism which he had promised to Louis XIV and to his younger sister, Minette? The Declaration caused such an outcry that Charles was forced to withdraw it, and the Test Acts that Parliament passed in order to exclude Catholics from public office were so successful that the tone and proposals in Sancroft's letter of 1681 are readily explicable.

One view of Charles's religious convictions:
> His religion was deism, or rather that which is called so; and if in his exile he went into that of Rome, the first was to be imputed to a complaisance for the company he was then obliged to keep, and the

last to a lazy diffidence in all other religions, upon a review of his past life and the near approach of an uncertain state.
From Memoirs of the Most Material Transactions of England by James Welwood
quoted in ENGLISH HISTORICAL DOCUMENTS, vol. 8 (1660–1714)
edited by A. Browning   Eyre & Spottiswoode, 1953   *p.900*

Another view:
> The watching bishops gathered round the bed. ... Ken ... implored him to receive the last rites of that Protestant communion of which, for the last few hours of life that remained, he was the head. The King thanked him, and declared his sorrow for his sins, but begged him with great gentleness to desist from his entreaties. Somehow, he knew now, he must keep them away. Beyond the crowded darkness of the room, swaying and choking, his spirit was following a clearer trail, moving across the wet woods of Boscobel and the starlit meadows towards Moseley, where in a plain upper chamber two candles burnt before an ancient and secret altar. Strangely, it was his little sister who was leading him there.
>
> KING CHARLES II
> *by Sir A. Bryant   Collins, 1960*   *pp.293–294*

The Declaration of Breda, 1660:
> And because the passion and uncharitableness of the times have produced several opinions in religion, by which men are engaged in parties and animosities against each other, which, when they shall hereafter unite in a freedom of conversation, will be composed or better understood, we do declare a liberty to tender consciences ...
>
> *JOURNALS OF THE HOUSE OF LORDS*, vol. 11   *pp.7–8*

Speech of Charles to Parliament, 1662:
> Gentlemen, I hear you are very zealous for the Church, and very solicitous and even jealous that there is not expedition enough used in that affair. I thank you for it, since, I presume, it proceeds from a good root of piety and devotion. But I must tell you I have the worst luck in the world, if, after all the reproaches of being a Papist, whilst I was abroad, I am suspected of being a Presbyterian now I am come home. I know you will not take it unkindly if I tell you that I am as zealous for the Church of England as any of you can be ... that I am as much in love with the Book of Common Prayer as you can wish, and have prejudice enough to those that do not love it; who, I hope, in time will be better informed and change their minds. And you may be confident, I do as much desire to see a uniformity settled as any amongst you. . . . I have transmitted the

Book of Common Prayer, with those alterations and additions which have been presented to me by the Convocation, to the House of Peers, with my approbation, that the Act of Uniformity may relate to it: so that I presume it will be shortly dispatched there. And when we have done all we can, the well settling that affair will require great prudence and discretion and the absence of all passion and precipitation.
JOURNALS OF THE HOUSE OF COMMONS, 1660–1667   p.377

The Act of Uniformity, 1662:
> I. . . . Be it enacted . . . That all and singular ministers [&c.] . . . shall be bound to say and use the Morning Prayer, Evening Prayer, celebration and administration of both the sacraments, and all other the public and common prayer . . . in the said book entitled, *The Book of Common Prayer* . . . according to the use of the Church of England. . . .
> III. And to the end that uniformity in the public worship of God . . . may be speedily effected, be it further enacted. . . . Every parson, vicar . . . shall . . . before the feast of St Bartholomew which shall be in the year of our Lord God one thousand six hundred and sixty and two, openly, publicly, and solemnly read the Morning and Evening Prayer . . . and after such reading thereof shall openly and publicly, before the congregation there assembled, declare his unfeigned assent and consent to the use of all things in the said book contained. . . .
> V. . . . that all and every person, who shall . . . neglect or refuse to do the same within the time aforesaid . . . shall *ipso facto* be deprived of all his spiritual promotions. . . .
> *STATUTES OF THE REALM*, vol. 5   *pp.364–370*

The Five Mile Act, 1665:
> . . . all such person and persons as shall take upon them to preach in any unlawful assembly, conventicle or meeting under colour or pretence of any exercise of religion, contrary to the laws and statutes of this kingdom, shall not at any time from and after 24th March 1665, unless only in passing on the road, come to be within five miles of any city, or town corporate, or borough that sends burgesses to Parliament, . . . upon forfeiture for every such offence the sum of £40 of lawful English money.
> *STATUTES OF THE REALM*, vol. 5   *p.575*

Letter from Archbishop Sancroft to Bishop Compton of London, 1681:
> His Majesty having yesternight in Council (to the great satisfaction and joy of us all) declared his royal will and pleasure that all papists and popish recusants throughout the realm be forthwith vigorously prosecuted, and the laws of the land made against them

effectually put in execution, to the end that by such wholesome severity (so seasonable and necessary at this time) they may by God's blessing upon his Majesty's pious intentions, and the endeavours of his good subjects in pursuance of the same, be either reduced into the bosom of the Church or driven out of the kingdom, I could not but immediately reflect how highly it concerns, and how well it may beseem me and my brethren, and all that are intrusted with the manage of any jurisdiction under us, to contribute all we can, and particularly what the laws of the land and the canons of the Church require of us, for the promoting and accomplishing (if it may be) so good a design, which tends so manifestly to the glory of God, the honour of his Majesty's government, the prosperity and flourishing estate of that excellent religion by the peculiar blessing of heaven established among us, and the quiet and tranquillity of the whole realm.

I have therefore thought fit at present (till other and further methods may be debated and resolved on) to require all the bishops within this province and every of them, and I do hereby require them, that those three canons against popish recusants agreed upon in the synod begun at London A.D. 1603, namely the lxvth, lxvith, and the cxivth be by them, and all that hold or exercise any jurisdiction under them, forthwith exactly observed and effectually put in use, considering how acceptable a service it will be to Almighty God to assist his Majesty's pious purpose herein, and on the other side how severe a punishment the last canon of the three appoints to those who shall neglect their duty herein, which will (I doubt not) without partiality or connivance be inflicted on them.

My Lord, my request to your lordship is that you will not only take notice of all this yourself, but cause a copy hereof, by you attested, to be transmitted to every bishop of this province in the name of

        Your affectionate brother,
        William Canterbury

April 9, 1681.

DOCUMENTARY ANNALS OF THE REFORMED CHURCH OF ENGLAND, vol. 2
by E. Cardwell   O.U.P., 1844   *pp.347–349*

Charles II and Roman Catholicism

What weight are we to give to Roman Catholicism in Charles II's life, and how were his attitudes to it formed? Readers are referred to Chapter Two for extracts from Charles's letters to his younger sister, 'Minette', which may provide a clue. The evidence from Clarendon and Pepys shows us the kind of Catholicism with which Charles came into contact. The person against whom Clarendon wrote was Hugh

Serenus Cressy, who had apostatized from the Church of England and became a Benedictine monk, yet retained, in Clarendon's eyes, compensating qualities. Did Charles think that this religion could be made the religion of England? Even the precise nature of the events of Charles's deathbed reception into the Roman Catholic Church remains open to question. The accounts printed here differ with regard to several important details. Both Barillon and Padre Mansuet, the Duke of York's chaplain, had their points of view and neither was in a position directly to be able to observe what took place. Which of them is more to be trusted as an impartial and an accurate witness?

Clarendon on Charles's years in exile:

> For my own part I have always had more kindness and esteem for the monks of that Order, I mean for those of the English Congregation, and have had more conversation with them, than any other religious of our nation. They are (very few excepted) all gentlemen, and of very good families (as Mr Cressy is) and of very civil and quiet natures . . . and they were very kind to all their banished countrymen in France and Flanders . . . I have been assured that they expressed more affection and duty to the King, and were more useful to him, even in assisting him with money in his greatest distresses, and performing other offices for him, than all other religious communities put together.
>
> *From Animadversions upon a Book Intituled Fanaticism Fanatically*
> *Imputed to the Catholic Church by Dr Stillingfleet and the Imputations*
> *refuted and retorted by S. C[ressy] by Edward Hyde, Earl of Clarendon*
> *quoted by David Lunn in HISTORY TODAY, vol. 25, 1975   p.232*

Pepys on Court Catholicism:

> The Queene coming by in her coach, going to her chapel at St James's (the first time it hath been ready for her), I crowded after her; and got up to the room where her closet is and there stood and saw the fine alter, ornaments and the fryers in their habits and the priests come in with their fine Copes. And many other very fine things. I heard their Musique too; which may be good, but it did not appear so to me, neither as to their manner of singing nor was it good Concord to my eares, whatever the matter was. . . . The Queene was there and some ladies. But Lord! what an odd thing it was for me to be in a crowd of people, here a footman, there a beggar, here a fine lady, there a zealous poor papist, and here a Protestant, two or three together, come to see the show. I was afeared of my pocket being picked very much. . . . And I see the papists have the wit, most of them, to bring cushions to kneel on, which I wanted, and was mighty troubled to kneel.
>
> THE DIARY OF SAMUEL PEPYS
> *edited by R. Latham and W. Matthews   G. Bell, 1970–1976*
> *vol. 3, p.202; vol. 8, p.588*

ON Monday, being the 2d. of February, the King rose early, saying, that he had not slept well the last Night: And about seven of the Clock, coming from his private Devotions, out of his Closet, fell down, (and scarce any sign of of Life remaining in him for the space of four Houres) of a Fit of an Apoplexy, but with the loss of sixteen Ounces of Blood, and other Aplications, came again to his Sences, and great Hopes were of his Recovery, till Thursday one of the Clock; so that at five, the Doctors being come before the Council, declared that the K--- was in great Danger; and on Friday, a quarter before twelve, he departed this Life. God have Mercy on his Soul.

P. M. A. C. F. came to the D. upon the Doctors telling him of the State of the K. and tould him that now was the time for him to take care of his Br. Soul, and that it was his Duty to tell him so: The D. with this Admonishment went to the K. and after some private Discourse, the K. uttered these Expressions, Oh B. how long have I wished——— but now help me; withal declaring that he would have Mr. H. who had preserved him in the Tree, and now hoped would preserve his Soul. Mr. Hud. was accordingly sent for, and desired to bring all Nessisaries for a dying Man, but he not having the blessed Sacrament by him, went to one of the Q. P. and telling him the Occasion, desired his Assistance to procure it, and to bring it to the back Stairs. The K. having notice that Mr. H. waited at the Door, desired to be in private, whereupon the Bps. and all the Nobles withdrew, the D. catching fast the Door, the Lords P. E. and F. were going out also, but the D. told them that they might stay. The K. seeing Mr. H. cryed out, *Almighty God, what good Planet governs me, that all my Life is Wonders and Miracles? When, O Lord, I consider my Infancy, my Exile, my Escape at Worcester, my Preservation in the Tree, with the Assistance of this good Father; and now to have him again to preserve my Soul: O Lord, my wonderful Restoration, my great Danger in the Late Conspiracy; and last of all, to be raised from Death to Life, and to have my Soul preserved by the Assistance of this Father, whom I see, O good Lord, that thou hast created for my Good.* The D. and Lords withdrew into the Closset for the space of an houre and half, then entring again the Room, the F. asked the K. whether he would be pleased to receive; he answered, *If I were worthy of it* ——— *Amen, Amen.* The F. remaining comforting and praying with him, he said, Father if I am worthy of it, I pray let me have it? The F. said it would be brought to him imediately, and asked his Leave to proceed with extream Unction, the K. reply'd, with all my Heart, the D. and Lords assisting at the time. Mr. H. was called to the Door, where he received the blessed Sacrament, and desiring the K. to compose himself to receive, he would fain have arose (but was perswaded to the contrary) saying, *Let me meet my heavenly Father in a better manner than lying on my back.* But being overruled, they continue in Prayer: Amongst others, the Father repeats an Act of Contrition, desiring the K. to repeat it word by word after him: Having made an end, the K. received with the greatest Expressions of Devotion imaginable: This being ended, they go on with the Prayers *de Anime*; that being done, the K. desired the Act of Contrition to be again repeated, saying, *O Lord, good God, when my Lips fail, let my Heart speak these Words Eternally, Amen.* The Bishops and Lords enter again the Room, and desire the K. to remember his last End, and to endeavour to make a good End; he said he had thought of it, and hoped he had made his Peace with God; they asked him whether he would receive, he said he would not; so persisting in Extolling the Q. and D. saying he was not sorry to leave the World, leaving so good a Brother to Rule behind him.

F I N I S.

An account of Charles II's death by Padre Mansuet, a Capuchin Friar

Report of Paul Barillon, the French Ambassador, on Charles II's death, 8–18 February 1685:

The duke of York, to whom I had given notice that all was ready, sent Chiffinch to receive and bring in Mr Huddleston. Soon after he said aloud, "The king wills that everybody should retire, except the earls of Bath and Feversham." The first was lord of the bedchamber, and the other was in waiting. The physicians went into a closet, the door of which was immediately shut, and Chiffinch brought Mr Huddleston in. The duke of York in presenting him said, "Sire, here is a man who saved your life, and is now come to save your soul." The king answered, "He is welcome." He afterwards confessed himself with great sentiments of devotion and repentance.

The count of Castel Melhor had taken care to have Huddleston instructed by a Portuguese monk of the barefooted Carmelites in what he had to say to the king on such an occasion, for of himself he was no great doctor; but the duke of York told me he acquitted himself very well in his function, and that he made the king formally promise to declare himself openly a Catholic if he recovered his health. He then received absolution, the communion and even the extreme unction. All this lasted about three-quarters of an hour. In the ante-chamber every one looked at another, but nobody said anything but by their eyes and in whispers. The presence of Lord Bath and Lord Feversham, who are Protestants, has satisfied the bishops a little; but the queen's women and the other priests saw so much going and coming that I do not think the secret can be long kept.

After the king of England received the communion his disorder became a little better. It is certain he spoke more intelligibly, and had more strength. We hoped that God was willing to work a miracle by restoring him; but the physicians judged his illness was not abated, and that he could not outlive the night. He nevertheless appeared much more easy and spoke with more feeling and understanding than he had done from ten at night to eight in the morning. He often spoke quite aloud to the duke of York in terms full of tenderness and friendship. He twice recommended to him the duchess of Portsmouth and the duke of Richmond. He recommended to him also all his other children. He made no mention of the duke of Monmouth, good or bad. He often expressed his confidence in the mercy of God. The bishop of Bath and Wells, who was his chaplain, read some prayers and spoke to him of God. The king showed by his head that he heard him. The bishop was not officious in saying anything particular to him, or proposing that he should make a profession of his faith. He was apprehensive of a refusal, but feared still more, as I believe, to irritate the duke of York.

The king of England was perfectly sensible the whole night, and spoke upon all things with great calmnes. At six o'clock in the morning he asked what hour it was, and said, "Open the curtains, that I may once more see day." He suffered great pain, and at seven o'clock they bled him in hopes that it might lessen his pain. At half an hour after eight he began to speak with great difficulty; at ten his senses were quite gone; and he died at noon without any struggle or convulsion. The new king retired to his apartment, was unanimously acknowledged, and then proclaimed.

From Sir John Dalrymple: Memoirs
quoted in ENGLISH HISTORICAL DOCUMENTS, *vol. 8 (1660–1714)*
edited by A. Browning   Eyre & Spottiswoode, 1953

The Economy

5

By what means did Charles II seek to promote the economy?
Protection or free trade?

To promote commerce and the economy, Charles II had only to 'keep up the merchant', according to the Duke of Newcastle. But how? The frequency with which this advice was dinned into the ears of rulers in this period has given rise to a special name, mercantilism, but so divided have both contemporary writers and historians been about its meaning, that it has become as valuable as the solemn promise of a Renaissance prince. The extracts printed below present a cross-section of differing opinions on how to 'keep up the merchant': by protection or by free trade. Adam Smith, advocating free trade in *The Wealth of Nations* was clear in his own mind about the meaning of mercantilism:

> Though the encouragement of exportation, and the discouragement of importation, are the two great engines by which the mercantile system proposes to enrich every country, yet with regard to some particular commodities, it seems to follow an opposite plan: to discourage exportation and to encourage importation. Its ultimate object, however, it pretends, is always the same, to enrich the country by an advantageous balance of trade.
>
> THE WEALTH OF NATIONS *(first pub. 1776)*
> *by Adam Smith, edited by W. B Todd   O.U.P., 1976*   *p.642*

Writers in Charles II's reign, however, were more muddled, and we must be careful not to impose a more rigid system on them than that which they actually believed.

The Duke of Newcastle, 1660:

> It is the merchant that only brings honey to the hive.... Therefore your Majesty will be pleased to keep up the merchant that can only fill your kingdom with riches, and so consequently enrich your Majesty; for if your kingdom be poor, where can your Majesty have it? Nowhere. Therefore your Majesty will be pleased to enrich your kingdom that neither your Majesty nor your subjects

may want, and that is done absolutely by the merchant and only by the merchant.
Bodleian Library, Oxford; Clarendon MSS 109, fol. 41
quoted in THE RESTORATION
by Joan Thirsk   Longman, 1976 p.115

Roger Coke:
As we give no encouragement to our industrious natives, so we utterly discourage all industrious foreigners from improving and increasing trade. . . .

And the French King so well understands how much it will conduce to the advantage of France to encourage the freedom of trade, by entertaining all sorts of foreign artificers, that in contradiction to all the ecclesiastical powers opposing it, he hath granted free liberty to all sorts of foreign artificers and merchants to exercise their consciences in all ports and places in his dominion, and to have churches allowed them with equal or more privileges than his natural subjects. Sure now it will be no ways prudent in us so to discourage any herein, as to be entertained by the French King, as well as Dutch.
From A Discourse of Trade by Roger Coke, 1670
quoted in THE RESTORATION
by Joan Thirsk   Longman, 1976 p.121

Carew Reynel:
We are come to this improvement that we are not so much by the indulgent care of rich men as by the wants of some ingenious persons forcing them to improve themselves for a livelihood. But what perfection should we arrive to if (in imitation of His Majesty and Royal Highness, who much encourage trade, ingenuity, and discoveries, even beyond any former princes) other great and rich persons would set about the work and private persons would get public spirits to labour after things so beneficial not only to the nation in general but to every man in particular. We take up our time about little businesses and it may be factious discourses when the whole profit of the nation, which is properly a nation of trade, lies unregarded. And half the charges that were spent in the last rebellion would have brought the gold of Guinea and riches of the Indies to us. . . .

As it is an advantage to have variety of manufactures, so also it is to have variety of husbandries, for the more several husbandries the ground is taken up with, the more every grain and commodity will vent one for another, and so advance the rate of land, produce greater profit and increase and maintain more people; but of all plantations at present, vineyards, orchards for cider, and tobacco plantations would be the most advantageous, especially tobacco; it

A British colony: Tangiers from the South West

sets an infinite [*sic*] of people on work, increaseth the rent of land, and returns great profit to the planter as can be proved beyond all exceptions, if time and occasion required.
*From The True English Interest by Carew Reynel, 1674
quoted in* THE RESTORATION
by Joan Thirsk   Longman, 1976   *pp.121–122*

An anonymous writer, 1680:
> Private interest is that many-headed monster, I am chiefly to encounter with, in which if any particular person shall take himself to be concerned, I shall desire him to consider, whether his own condition would not be more truly honourable and safe under more open methods of trade? I shall pray him to look into the nature of mere private interest, which, if he do, he must confess it the same principle that leads men into cheats, thefts, and all those other base, merciless and execrable villanies, which render the actors criminous, and odious by the sufferings and injuries they bring upon others.
>
> Then if any man's particular way of gain be so prejudicial to trade, as to occasion the continual beggary of thousands of his countrymen, is not this more than equally mischievous to so many thousand thefts? But what if this beggary must unavoidably cause many thousand actual thefts, nay murders and enormities of all kinds, and as it grows more universal, must bring the nation into an impotent and indefensible weakness? Have we any amongst us that will be yet tenacious of such ways of gain? Will they tell us that they are not punishable by any laws in force? 'tis pity they are not.

So there was a time when in old Rome, there was no direct law against parricide: but that they may no longer shelter themselves under this umbrage, it were highly necessary that laws were made to control them, and to remove all obstructions in our trade.
From Britannia Languens, or A Discourse of Trade
quoted in EARLY ENGLISH TRACTS ON COMMERCE
by J. R. McCulloch   Cambridge, Economic History Society, 1952
pp.287–288

Richard Baxter, 1696:
When most tenants fifty years ago sat on the old rents, perhaps some one landlord set his land on the rack rent from year to year, and was hardly spoken of for it by all the country. If another come and buy his land and then raise it higher and set that at £50 or £60 which he set at £40, and that at £40 which he set at £30, and that at £4 which he set at £2 or £3, may not I justly petition that the poor people may have the clemency of their former rack which they called *cruelty*? This is no rare case. Few scruple raising rents to as much as they can get, when poor men, rather than beg and have no dwelling, will promise more than they can pay; and then, with care and toil, make shift as long as they can; and then run away and do so in another country. And so the gentlemen lose more by their *racking* than they get, whereas if they would abate a third part, and let their tenants live a comfortable life, they might have their rents constantly paid, and have the people's love, and partake of the comforts of those that are benefited or comforted by them.

To this end I humbly entreat you, gentlemen, to retrench your needless and sinful charges for superfluities, prodigality, and fleshy lust. That you may not need so much to feed your sin as will not leave you enough to discharge your duty to God and to the poor. Cannot you live as healthfully and decently with fewer dishes, and less variety, and less cost and curiosity, and less ostentation, attendance and pomp? Do not your tables and your furniture speak unbelief and contempt of Christ?
From The Reverend Richard Baxter's Last Treatise
quoted in THE RESTORATION
by Joan Thirsk   Longman, 1976   *pp.134–135*

Charles's economic policy

Charles II was mesmerized, not by France, despite the Whig historians, but by the Dutch, who provided the best example of commercial and industrial success in Europe and were Britain's chief rival. The Navigation Act of 1660, Charles's intimate letters to his sister about the Dutch, his encouragement of companies and his interest in the Navy can be looked at in this light. The foundation of colonies, too, looked at in conjunction with Carew Reynel's proposals, can be seen as an attempt to break away from areas of Dutch control and from current British obsessions. Ultimately, however, there was a limit to what the Government could do to aid the economy, already vigorous before 1660, and Charles II probably did more good by interfering less than did the most notable exponent of protectionism, Louis XIV.

The Navigation Act, 1660:
> An Act for the encouraging and increasing of shipping and navigation.
>
> For the increase of shipping and encouragement of the navigation of this nation wherein, under the good providence and protection of God, the wealth, safety and strength of this kingdom is so much concerned; be it enacted by the King's most excellent Majesty, and by the Lords and Commons in this present Parliament assembled, and by the authority thereof, that from and after the first day of December one thousand six hundred and sixty, and from thenceforward, no goods or commodities whatsoever shall be imported into or exported out of any lands, islands, plantations or territories to his Majesty belonging or in his possession, or which may hereafter belong unto or be in the possession of his Majesty, his heirs and successors in Asia, Africa or America, in any other ship ... but in such ships or vessels as do truly and without fraud belong only to the people of England or Ireland, dominion of Wales or town of Berwick-upon-Tweed, or are of the built of and belonging to any the said lands, islands, plantations or territories, as the proprietors and right owners thereof, and whereof the master and three-fourths of the mariners at least are English.
>
> And it is further enacted by the authority aforesaid, that no goods or commodities that are of foreign growth, production or manufacture, and which are brought into England, Ireland, Wales, the islands of Guernsey and Jersey, or town of Berwick-upon-Tweed, in English-built shipping, or other shipping belonging to some of the aforesaid places, and navigated by English mariners, as aforesaid, shall be shipped or brought from any other place or places, country or countries, but only from those of the said growth, production or manufacture, or from those ports where the said goods, and commodities can only, or are, or usually have been, first shipped for transportation, and from no other places or countries.
>
> *STATUTES OF THE REALM*, vol. 5   *p.246*

Samuel Pepys, 26 August 1666:
> Penn and I by coach to White-hall and there stayed till the King and Cabinet was met in the green Chamber, and then were called

in; and there the King begun with me, to hear how the victualls of the fleet stood; I did in a long discourse tell him and the rest (the Duke of York, Lord Chancellor, Lord Treasurer, both the Secretarys, Sir G. Carteret, and Sir W. Coventry) how it stood; wherein they seemed satisfied, but press mightily for more supplies; and the letter of the Generals, which was read, did lay their not going, or too soon returning from the Duch coast, this next bout, to the want of victuals. Then they proceeded to the enquiry after the fireships; and did all very superficially – and without any severity at all. But however, I was in pain, after we came out, to know how I had done – and hear, well enough. But however, it shall be a caution to me to prepare myself against a day of inquisition.

THE DIARY OF SAMUEL PEPYS, vol. 7
edited by R. Latham and W. Matthews   G. Bell, 1970–1976   p.260

John Houghton, 1682:
Since His Majesty's most happy Restoration the whole land hath been fermented and stirred up by the profitable hints it hath received from the Royal Society, by which means parks have been disparked, commons enclosed, woods turned to arable, and pasture lands improved by clover, sainfoin, turnips, coleseed, purslane, and many other good husbandries, so that the food of cattle is increased as fast, if not faster, than the consumption, and by these means, although some particular lands may fall, I strongly persuade myself that altogether the rent of the kingdom is far greater than ever it was.

From A Collection of Letters for the Improvement of Husbandry and Trade
quoted in THE RESTORATION
by Joan Thirsk   Longman, 1976   pp.133–134

Letter of Charles II to Madame, 2 June 1664:
Sir George Downing is come out of Holland, and I shall now be very busy upon that matter. The States keep a great bragging and noise, but I believe, when it comes to it, they will look twice before they leap. I never saw so great an appetite to a war as is, in both town and country, especially in the Parliament men, who, I am confident, would pawn their estates to maintain a war. But all this shall not govern me, for I will look merely [to] what is just and best for the honour and good of England, and will be very steady in what I resolve, and if I be forced to a war, I shall be ready with as good ships and men as ever was seen, and leave the rest to God.

From Madame by Julia Cartwright, 1894
quoted in LETTERS, SPEECHES AND DECLARATIONS OF KING CHARLES II
edited by Sir A. Bryant   Cassell, 1935   p.159

Samuel Pepys

Charles to Madame, 20 June 1664:
> I see you are as hot upon setting up an East India Company at Paris as we are here upon our Guinea trade. We are now sending eight ships thither, to the value of £50,000, and I have given them a convoy of a man-of-war, lest the Dutch in those parts might do them much harm in revenge for our taking the fort of Cape Verde, which will be of great use to our trade.
>
> *From Madame by Julia Cartwright, 1894*
>   quoted in LETTERS, SPEECHES AND DECLARATIONS OF KING CHARLES II
>   *edited by Sir A. Bryant   Cassell, 1935*   *p.159*

(This letter conflicts with the story of Charles's reply to the Dutch Ambassador's protest over the incident: 'And pray what is Cape Verde? – a stinking place.')

Charles to Madame, 23 August 1664:
> My Lord Holles will give you a true state of that business, wherein you may find how much the Hollanders are in the wrong, I mean

the two Companies of the East and West India, against whom my complaints are, and the States hitherto have given them more countenance and assistance than they ought to have done. I must confess I would like to know what I may expect from France, in case the Hollanders should refuse me all sort of reason and justice, for upon that, I must take my measures accordingly.

From Madame by Julia Cartwright, 1894
quoted in LETTERS, SPEECHES AND DECLARATIONS OF KING CHARLES II
edited by Sir A. Bryant   Cassell, 1935   *p.163*

Letter of Charles II to the East India Company, 14 September 1676:
Whereas we are humbly informed that Edmund Halley, a student of Queen's College in Oxford (who for several years hath been a diligent observer of the Planets and Stars), hath an intention in order to the making observations for rectifying and finishing the Celestial Globe, to pass and remain for some time in the Isle of St. Helena (which place he conceives very fit and proper for such a design). We being graciously willing to give all encouragement and protection to whatever may tend to the improvement of navigation and be beneficial to the public, have thought fit hereby most particularly to recommend him to you, that you will give order, that he, his friend and their necessaries may be transported to the said island upon the first of your ships which shall go thither, and that he be received and entertained there and have such assistance and countenance from your officers as he may stand in need of. And we not doubting of your readiness to contribute on your parts what fairly may be expected for his encouragement to proceed in so useful an undertaking, we bid you farewell.

From PUBLIC RECORDS OFFICE; STATE PAPERS
44/42, fol. 34
quoted in LETTERS, SPEECHES AND DECLARATIONS OF KING CHARLES II
edited by Sir A. Bryant   Cassell, 1935   *p.286*

Letter of Charles II to Lord Baltimore, 2 April 1681:
Right trusty, etc.... Whereas by our letters patent bearing date the 4th day of March last past we have been graciously pleased out of our royal bounty and the singular regard which we have to the merits and services of Sir William Penn, deceased, to give and grant to our trusty, etc.... William Penn, Esq., son and heir to the said Sir William Penn, a certain tract of land in America by the name of Pennsylvania, as the same is bounded on the east by Delaware River from twelve miles distant northwards of New Castle town unto the forty-third degree of northern latitude, if the said river doth extend so far northwards, and if the said river shall not extend so far northward, then by the said river so far as it doth extend, and from the head of the said river the eastern bounds to be

determined by a meridian line to be drawn from the head of the said river unto the said forty-third degree; the said Province to extend westwards five degrees in longitude to be computed from the said eastern bounds and to be bounded on the north by the beginning of the forty-third degree of northern latitude, and on the south by a circle drawn at twelve miles distance from New Castle northwards and westwards unto the beginning of the fortieth degree of northern latitude, and then by a straight line westwards to the limit of longitude above mentioned, as by our said letters patent doth particularly appear. And to the end that all due encouragement be given to the said William Penn in the settlement of a plantation within the said country, we do hereby recommend him his deputies and officers employed by him, to your friendly aid and assistance, willing and requiring you to do him all the offices of good neighbourhood and amicable correspondence which may tend to the mutual benefit of our subjects within our provinces under your respective proprieties. And more especially we do think fit that in order hereunto you do appoint with all convenient speed some person or persons who may in conjunction with the agent or agents of the said William Penn make a true division and separation of the said provinces of Maryland and Pennsylvania, according to the bounds and degree of northern latitude expressed in our said letters patent, by settling and fixing certain landmarks, where they shall appear to border upon each other for the preventing and according all doubts and controversies that may otherwise happen concerning the same....

From *PUBLIC RECORDS OFFICE; STATE PAPERS 389/4, fol. 164v–165*
quoted in LETTERS, SPEECHES AND DECLARATIONS OF KING CHARLES II
edited by Sir A. Bryant   Cassell, 1935   pp.322–323

It is impossible to disentangle finance and the economy from foreign policy, religion and the advancement of science, though it does not follow that all Charles II's policies had an economic motive. Readers must make their own judgment after reading the extracts elsewhere in this book: Charles's statement of policy to Louis XIV regarding Anglo-Dutch rivalry; his proposals for religious toleration, which become more understandable if seen in the light of Roger Coke's suggestion (see page 54); and the foundation charter of the Royal Society.

6 Science, the Arts and Society

How significant a part did Charles II play in the development of science, the arts and social morality?

Social morality: a double standard

Attitudes to social morality and to sport and entertainment were closely interwoven in the mind of the Duke of Newcastle, an old-fashioned Cavalier, who advised the King to return to what he considered to have been the golden age of Elizabeth, when England was merry and men kept their station in life. How closely Charles followed this advice can be seen from the following extracts, but his actions were by no means entirely consistent. The ruling élite appear to have tried harder than the King himself to restore ceremony and the social order, and Charles seems – more than any monarch for centuries before or after him – to have applied to himself that merry-making which Newcastle reserved to the lower orders. However, Charles's patronage of the first rhymed heroic play in English (Orrery's *The Generall*) seems to conflict with his apparent preference for comedy. Perhaps the Court ladies, who liked tragedies, had some influence over him. Or he may not have been entirely indifferent to the pomp that should surround a king. Heroic poetry and the embellishment of Windsor Castle in continental style may have been inspired by envy of the power of his cousin, Louis XIV.

The Duke of Newcastle on ceremony and order, 1660:
> ... ceremony and order, with force, governs all, both in peace and war, and keeps every man and everything within the circle of their own conditions. Nay, very bear baiting without ceremony and order would be in more confusion than it is, and many such like things. Therefore, your Majesty will be pleased to keep it up strictly in your own person and court, to be a precedent to the rest of your nobles and not to make yourself too cheap by too much familiarity, which, as the proverb says, breeds contempt. But when you appear to shew yourself gloriously to your people, like a God – for the Holy Writ says, we have called you gods – and when the

The Royal Chapel, Windsor Castle; from the watercolour by C. Wild

people see you thus, they will down of their knees.... So if your Majesty please to speak to your Heralds, to set down the ceremony and order for all degrees of your nobility, as for barons, viscounts, earls, marquises and dukes, and to have it printed, and so for all the great officers, their ceremony and order, and not any to entrench one upon another, but to keep only what is right and due for their places and dignities. It's one thing, none under the degree of a baroness can have carpets by her bed, and she but one or two at the most. And now every Turkey merchant's wife will have all her floor over with carpets. So now every citizen's wife will have six horses in her coach, which is most unfitting. They say the ways are so foul when 'tis their pride, for I am sure when I was a boy, Gilbert, the great Earl of Shrewsbury, never went but with four horses in his coach and those of meaner degrees but with two horses, and travelled many hundred miles, and the ways as foul as they are now. The king of Spain allows nobody six horses but himself. This your Majesty will rectify very easily. So to make no difference between great ladies and citizens' wives in apparel is abominable. No, they should go to their little black velvet caps, small gold chains, and little ruffs, as they were in my time, and their apprentices in their round black caps. But this must take a little time, for fear of offending too fast, until your Majesty be well settled in your saddle – and when any of these orders are violated, to be brought into your Marshall's court and there punished, which court, though it was spoken against in Parliament, is a most excellent court, for it keeps up ceremony and order, so the court be kept within his bounds....

Bodleian Library, Oxford; Clarendon MSS 109, fol. 52–54
quoted in THE RESTORATION
by Joan Thirsk   Longman, 1976   *pp.156–157*

The Duke of Newcastle on recreations and festivals, 1660:

First for London, Paris Garden will hold good for the meaner people. Then for several playhouses, as there were five at least in my time ... but five or six playhouses is enough for all sorts of people's diversion and pleasure in that kind. Then puppet plays there will be to please them, besides as also dancers of the ropes, with jugglers and tumblers, besides strange sights of beasts, birds, monsters, and many other things, which several sorts of music and dancing and all the old holidays with their mirth and rites set up again, feasting daily will be in merry England, for England is so plentiful of all provision that if we do not eat them, they will eat us, so we feast in our own defence....

May games, Morris dances, the Lord of the May and Lady of the May, the fool and the Hoby Horse must not be forgotten, also Whitsun Lord and Lady, thrashing of hens at Shrove Tide, carols and wassails at Christmas, with good plum porridge and pies which now are forbidden as profane, ungodly things, wakes, fairs and markets maintains commerce and trade, and after evening prayer every Sunday and Holy Day the country people, with their fresher lasses, to trip on the town green about the maypole to the louder bagpipe there to be refreshed with their ale and cakes ... these divertisments will amuse the people's thoughts and keep them in harmless actions which will free your Majesty from faction and rebellion.

Bodleian Library, Oxford; Clarendon MSS 109, fol. 74–75
quoted in THE RESTORATION
by Joan Thirsk   Longman, 1976   *p.184*

Charles II and Roger Boyle, Earl of Orrery (The extracts below concern the playwright and the circumstances surrounding the writing of *The Generall*. These extracts are, respectively, from Orrery's first biographer and from Charles II, writing to Orrery.):

King Charles was the first who put my lord upon writing plays, which his majesty did upon occasion of a dispute that arose in his royal presence about writing plays in rhyme: some affirmed it was not to be done; others said it would spoil the fancy to be so confined, but the Lord Orrery was of another opinion; and his majesty being willing a trial should be made, commanded his lordship to employ some of his leisure that way, which my lord readily did.

I will now tell you, that I have read your first play, which I like very well, and do intend to bring it upon the stage, as soon as my Company have their new stage in order, that the scenes may be worthy the words they are to set forth ...

From The Impact of Charles II on Restoration Literature by James Sutherland
quoted in RESTORATION AND EIGHTEENTH-CENTURY LITERATURE. ESSAYS IN HONOUR OF ALAN DUGALD MCKILLOP
edited by Carroll Camden   Univ. of Chicago Press, 1963   pp.258–263

The King's sports; (1) Tennis:

Walking through the White Hall I heard the King was gone to play at tennis, so I down to the new tennis court, and saw him and Sir Arthur Slingsby play against my Lord of Suffolk and my Lord Chesterfield. The King beat three, and lost two sets, they all, and he particularly, playing well, I thought.

From The Diary of Samuel Pepys, 28 December 1663
quoted in CHARLES II
by Christopher Falkus   Weidenfeld & Nicolson, 1972   p.83

(2) Pall Mall:

>   Here a well-polished Mall gives us the joy
>   To see our Prince his matchless force employ;
>   He does but touch the flying ball,
>   And 'tis already half the Mall;
>   And such a fury from his arm has got,
>   As if from smoking culverin 'twere shot.

Edmund Waller, quoted in CHARLES II
by Christopher Falkus   Weidenfeld & Nicolson, 1972   p.83

(3) Horses and hunting:

I have had very good sport here [Newmarket] since Monday last, both by hunting and horse races. L'Abbé Pregnani is here, and wonders very much at the pleasure everyone takes at the races. He was so weary with riding from Audley End [the Queen's residence] hither, to see the foot match, as he is scarce recovered yet. I have been a fox hunting this day and am very weary. Yet the weather is so good, as my brother has persuaded me to see his fox hounds run tomorrow ...

From Madame by Julia Cartwright, 1894
quoted in LETTERS, SPEECHES AND DECLARATIONS OF KING CHARLES II
edited by Sir A. Bryant   Cassell, 1935   p.231

A tennis match

Pall Mall

The King's style at Newmarket, 1682:
> The King was so much pleased with the country, and so great a lover of the diversions which that place did afford, that he let himself down from majesty to the very degree of a country gentleman. He mixed himself amongst the crowd, allowed every man to speak to him that pleased; went a-hawking in the mornings, to cock matches or foot races in the afternoons (if there were no horse races), and to plays in the evenings acted by very ordinary Bartholomew Fair comedians.
>
> *Sir John Reresby, quoted in* CHARLES II
> *by Christopher Falkus   Weidenfeld & Nicolson, 1972*   *p.192*

Manners, morals and conversation

The two extracts below present Charles II as a reformer. When allowance has been made for the vested interests of the two writers, is his such an unconvincing posture? Though Clarendon was the first non-Whig historian of his age, he was not ultra-Tory, and he reports the words of Charles II himself (in a speech to Parliament on 19 May 1662). Dryden was a convert to Catholicism and a propagandist for the Court. Was he right to say that Charles was responsible for the reform of conversation? He went on to argue that the example of the King's epigrams inspired a host of amateurs, 'ambitious to distinguish themselves from the herd of gentlemen', to attempt a poem or a play, rather than 'sit down quietly with their estates'.

Clarendon on the decline of morals:
> The relation between masters and servants had been long since dissolved by the Parliament, that their army might be increased by the prentices against their masters' consent, and that they might have intelligence of the secret meetings and transactions in those houses and families which were not devoted to them; from whence issued the foulest treacheries and perfidiousness that were ever practised. And the blood of the master was frequently the price of the servant's villany. ...
>
> 'He [Charles II] could not but observe that the whole nation seemed to him a little corrupted in their excess of living. All men spend much more in their clothes, in their diet, in all their expenses, than they had used to do. He hoped it had only been the excess of joy after so long sufferings that had transported him and them to those other excesses, but, he desired them, 'that they might all take heed that the continuance of them did not indeed corrupt their natures. He did believe that he had been that way very faulty himself; he promised that he would reform, and that if they would join with him in their several capacities, they would by their examples do more good, both in city and country, than any new laws would do.' He said many other good things that pleased

them, and no doubt he intended all he said, but the ways and expedients towards good husbandry were nowhere pursued. ...
THE LIFE OF EDWARD, EARL OF CLARENDON, vol. I
by himself Oxford, *1857* pp.*306 and 576–577*

Dryden on the reform of conversation:
> The desire of imitating so great a pattern first awakened the dull and heavy spirits of the English from their natural reservedness; loosened them from their stiff forms of conversation, and made them easy and pliant to each other in discourse. Thus, insensibly, our way of living became more free; and the fire of the English wit, which was being stifled under a constrained, melancholy way of breeding, began first to display its force, by mixing the solidity of our nation with the air and gaiety of our neighbours.

JOHN DRYDEN: ESSAYS, vol. I
edited by James Kinsley O.U.P., *1958* *p.176*

According to Rochester, Charles himself 'never said a foolish thing'. The King seems, however, to have wanted at one time to destroy the art of good conversation, since he ordered the suppression of coffee houses. These, however, were often places of seditious talk, and, at a time of acute political crisis, they were as politically dangerous to the Government as race meetings had been under the Protectorate.

The advancement of science

What credit can Charles be given for the spirit of enquiry that led Samuel Pepys, for example, into the examination of old concepts? This spirit may not have been so prevalent as later historians would lead us to expect, and its outcome, as the proceedings of the Royal Society indicate, may not always have been entirely enlightened. The frequent impracticality of these White Knights was to give much ammunition to Swift's satire in *Gulliver's Travels*. On the other hand, a historian of the Great Fire of London, Walter Bell, has written: 'London as it was created after the Fire owed more ... to King Charles II than to Sir Christopher Wren. His was the active, agitating mind. His hand was seen everywhere.'

Samuel Pepys's reflections on the Ark, c. 1684:
> Noah's Ark must needs be made of some extraordinary timber and plank, that could remain good after having been an hundred years in building, whereas our thirty new ships are some of them rotten within less than five. Moreover Mr Shere computes from its dimensions that six months would have sufficed to have built what Moses assigns an hundred years for. And enquire also how carpenters and caulkers came to be found if she was the first ship; what account could be given of all that ado for the preserving of

John Dryden

one little family that would of course have the curiosity of coming to see this great work; and lastly how they all agreed (contrary to all human practice in like cases of distresses, and particularly that of the *Gloucester* and the burning of London within my own observation) to see this means of safety enjoyed by so few persons and oxen and asses, suffering the universality of mankind to perish without contention for a share in it.

SAMUEL PEPYS'S NAVAL MINUTES
  edited by J. R. Tanner   Navy Records Society, 1926   *pp.205–206*

The Royal Society, 1669:
  This Royal Academy took its origin from some philosophers of London, and was restored in the reign of King Charles II, who (besides his own inclination) in order to encourage the genius of men of quality (who, at the time that there was no court in this kingdom, applied themselves diligently to such studies) estab-

lished and confirmed it, making himself in fact its founder by granting it the most ample privileges, which are recorded in a book ratified by the king, the duke of York and Prince Rupert. This institution is governed by a council, consisting of twenty members elected out of the whole body of the society, the head of which is the president, at present the earl of Brouncker, who, sitting on a seat in the middle of the table of the assembly, has a large silver mace with the royal arms lying before him, with which it is customary for the mace-bearer or the porter of the academy to walk before him. Persons of every nation and religion and profession are admitted among the academicians, and they are under no other obligation than to swear to the observance of the statutes, and to attend the meetings as often as is in their power (especially those for the election of officers) to promote its interests, and not to do anything to its prejudice.

At their meetings no precedence or distinction of place is observed, except by the president and secretary. The first is in the middle of the table, and the latter at the head of it, on his left hand, the other academicians taking their seats indifferently on benches of wood with backs to them arranged in two rows. And if anyone enters unexpectedly after the meeting has begun everyone remains seated, nor is his salutation returned except by the president alone, who acknowledges it by an inclination of the head, that he may not interrupt the person who is speaking on the subject or experiment proposed by the secretary.... Neither are opposite opinions maintained with obstinacy, but with temper, the language of civility and moderation being always adopted amongst them, which renders them so much the more praiseworthy as they are a society composed of persons of different nations....

The cabinet, which is under the care of Dr Robert Hooke, a man of genius and of much esteem in experimental matters, was founded by Daniel Colwall, now treasurer of the academy, and is full of the greatest rarities, brought from the most distant parts, such as quadrupeds, birds, fishes, serpents, insects, shells, feathers, seeds, minerals, and many petrifactions, mummies and gums. And every day, in order to enrich it still more, the academicians contribute everything of value which comes into their hands, so that in time it will be the most beautiful, the largest, and the most curious in respect of natural productions that is anywhere to be found. Amongst these curiosities the most remarkable are an ostrich whose young were always born alive, an herb which grew in the stomach of a thrush, and the skin of a moor, tanned, with the beard and hair white. But more worthy of observation than all the rest is a clock whose movements are derived from the vicinity of a loadstone; and it is so adjusted as to

The Castlemaine Globe, said to have been used by Charles II

discover the distance of countries at sea by the longitude. Towards this the planets or satellites of Jupiter are of great service, by the observation of whose eclipses (these succeeding one another almost every day) they are studying to find out a method of forming astronomical tables in order to discover the true meridians of the earth, for the different meridians will be shown by the

Charles II and the Royal Society

different hours at which they will happen, when observed at different places, beginning from the east and proceeding westward.

From Travels of Cosimo the Third by L. Megalotti
quoted in ENGLISH HISTORICAL DOCUMENTS, vol. 8 (1660–1714)
edited by A. Browning   Eyre & Spottiswoode, 1953   pp.481–482

Royal proclamation on the rebuilding of London, 13 September 1666:
And if . . . some obstinate and refractory persons will presume to erect such buildings as they shall think fit, upon pretence that the

Rebuilt London: 'Entrance to the Fleet River' *by Samuel Scott*

ground is their own, and that they may do with it what they please, such their obstinacy shall not prevail to the public prejudice: but we do hereby require the Lord Mayor, and the other magistrates of the City of London, in their several limits, to be very watchful in such cases. ...

... the woeful experience in this late heavy visitation hath sufficiently convinced all men of the pernicious consequences which have attended the building with timber, and even with stone itself, and the notable benefit of brick, which in so many places hath resisted and even extinguished the fire: and we do therefore hereby declare our express will and pleasure, that no man whatsoever shall presume to erect any house or building, great or small, but of brick or stone; and if any man shall do the contrary, the next magistrate shall forthwith cause it to be pulled down, and such further course shall be taken for his punishment as he deserves. And we suppose that the notable benefit many men have received from those cellars, which have been well and strongly arched, will persuade most men, who build good houses, to practise that good husbandry by arching all convenient places.

We do declare that Fleet Street, Cheapside, Cornhill, and all other eminent and notorious streets, shall be of such a breadth as may, with God's blessing, prevent the mischief that one side may suffer if the other be on fire; which was the case lately in Cheapside; the precise breadth of which several streets shall be, upon advice with the Lord Mayor and aldermen, shortly published, with many other particular orders and rules, which cannot yet be adjusted. In the meantime we resolve, though all streets cannot be of equal breadth, yet none shall be so narrow as to make the passage uneasy or inconvenient, especially towards the waterside. Nor will we suffer any lanes or alleys to be erected, but where, upon mature deliberation, the same shall be found absolutely necessary; except such places shall be set aside, which shall be designed only for buildings of that kind, and from whence no public mischief may probably arise.

HISTORICAL CHARTERS AND DOCUMENTS OF THE CITY OF LONDON
by W. de G. Birch   Whiting, 1884 *pp.224–227*

Conclusions 7

'The most skilful and unscrupulous politician of his age'. How true is this of Charles II?

If politics is the art of the possible, the word politician usually has a pejorative meaning: someone who applies mere tactics to short-term objectives in his conduct of the State. By contrast, a statesman has principles and a strategy, both of which he adheres to, despite all opposition and difficulties. It is commonly assumed that astuteness and a politician go together like bacon and eggs, that he will be, to borrow a seventeenth-century word, a wit – someone who is too clever by half. When a politician starts to talk, we watch his shifty feet and slip back a mental safety catch.

Was Charles II statesman or politician? Our answer will depend on how we define these terms. Did he have any principles which he was not prepared to forego? Was he more skilful and unscrupulous than his two closest rivals, Shaftesbury and Louis XIV? On all these questions there is conflicting evidence, and answers, especially on the Treaty of Dover and the Exclusion Crisis, can only be made by reference to the preceding chapters as well as to what follows.

Charles II in 1685

A reading of the judgment on Charles by Lord Macaulay, the great Whig historian, reveals the extent to which he was dependent on the views of the King's contemporaries. Two of these contemporaries must, however, be read with particular caution: Welwood, Charles's enemy, and Burnet, the disappointed cleric, both of whom wrote long after the King's death. But both obituaries have been so influential in forming subsequent opinion that they cannot be ignored.

James Welwood:
> He had read but little, yet he had a good taste of learning and would reason nicely upon most sciences. The mechanics were one of his peculiar talents, especially the art of building and working of ships, which nobody understood better, nor if he had lived would

have carried it farther. He had a strong laconic way of expression, and a genteel, easy and polite way of writing; and when he had a mind to lay aside the king, which he often did in select companies of his own, there were a thousand irresistible charms in his conversation. He loved money only to spend it, and would privately accept of a small sum paid to himself in lieu of a far greater to be paid into the Exchequer.

He loved not business and sought every occasion to avoid it, which was one reason that he passed so much of his time with his mistresses; yet when necessity called him none of his Council could reason more closely upon matters of state, and he would often by fits outdo his ministers in application and diligence. No age produced a greater master in the art of dissimulation, and yet no man was less upon his guard, or sooner deceived in the sincerity of others. If he had any one fixed maxim of government it was to play one party against another, to be thereby the more master of both; and no prince understood better how to shift hands upon every change of the scene. To sum up his character, he was dexterous in all the arts of insinuation, and had acquired so great an ascendant over the affections of his people, in spite of all the unhappy measures he had taken, that it may in some sense be said he died opportunely for England, since if he had lived it is probable we might in compliance with him have complimented ourselves out of all the remains of liberty, if he had had but a mind to be master of them, which it is but charity to believe he had not, at least immediately before his death.

From James Welwood: Memoirs
quoted in ENGLISH HISTORICAL DOCUMENTS, vol. 8 (1660–1714)
edited by A. Browning   Eyre & Spottiswoode, 1953   p.900

Burnet's obituary of Charles:

Thus lived and died king Charles the second. He was the greatest instance in history of the various revolutions of which any one man seemed capable. He was bred up the first twelve years of his life with the splendour that became the heir of so great a crown. After that he passed through eighteen years in great inequalities, unhappy in the war, in the loss of his father, and of the crown of England. Scotland did not only receive him, though upon terms hard of digestion, but made an attempt upon England for him, though a feeble one. He lost the battle of Worcester with too much indifference: and then he shewed more care of his person than became one who had so much at stake.... He got at last out of England: but he had been obliged to so many, who had been faithful to him, and careful of him, that he seemed afterwards to resolve to make an equal return to them all, and finding it not so easy to reward them as they deserved, he forgot them all alike....

His ill conduct in the first Dutch war, and those terrible calamities of the plague and fire of London, with that loss and reproach he suffered by the insult at Chatham, made all people conclude there was a curse upon his government. His throwing the public hatred at that time upon lord Clarendon was both unjust and ingrateful. And when his people had brought him out of all his difficulties upon his entering into the triple alliance, his selling that to France, and his entering on the second Dutch war with as little colour as he had for the first, his beginning it with the attempt on the Dutch Smyrna fleet, the shutting up the exchequer, and his declaration for toleration, which was a step for the introduction of popery, was such a chain of black actions, flowing from blacker designs, that it amazed those who had known all this. . . .

His person and temper, his vices as well as his fortunes, did resemble the character that we have given us of Tiberius so much, that it were easy to draw the parallel between them. Tiberius his banishment, and his coming afterwards to reign, makes the comparison in that respect come pretty near. His hating of business, and his love of pleasures, his raising of favourites and trusting them entirely, and his pulling them down and hating them excessively, his art of covering deep designs, particularly of revenge, with an appearance of softness, brings them so near a likeness, that I did not wonder much to observe the resemblance of their face and person. At Rome I saw one of the last statues made for Tiberius, after he had lost his teeth; but bating the alteration which that made, it was so like king Charles, that prince Borghese, and signior Dominico to whom it belonged, did agree with me in thinking that it looked like a statue made for him.

HISTORY OF MY OWN TIME, vol. 2
edited by O. Airy   O.U.P., 1897–1900   *pp.466–467, 471, 470*

Clarendon and Evelyn were kinder, in that they blamed Charles's associates, though much the same picture of the King's character emerges.

Edward Hyde, Earl of Clarendon, on Charles II:

Most men [i.e. in the Royalist party] were affected and more grieved and discontented for any honour and preferment which they saw conferred upon another man than for being disappointed in their own particular expectations; and looked upon every obligation bestowed upon another man, how meritorious soever, as upon a reproach to them, and an upbraiding of their want of merit.

This unhappy temper and constitution of the royal party, with whom he had always intended to have made a firm conjunction against all accidents and occurrences which might happen at home or from abroad, did wonderfully displease and trouble the king, and with the other perplexities which are mentioned before, did so break his mind, and had that operation upon his spirits that, finding he could not propose any such method to himself, by which he might extricate himself out of those many difficulties and labyrinths in which he was involved, nor expedite those important matters which depended upon the good will and dispatch of the Parliament, which would proceed by its own rules, and with its accustomed formalities, he grew more disposed to leave all things to their natural course and God's providence, and, by degrees, unbent his mind from the knotty and ungrateful part of his business, grew more remiss in his application to it, and indulged to his youth and appetite that license and satisfaction that it desired, and for which he had opportunity enough, and could not be without ministers abundant for any such negotiations, the time itself, and the young people thereof of either sex having been educated in all the liberty of vice without reprehension or restraint.

THE LIFE OF EDWARD, EARL OF CLARENDON, vol. I
by himself Oxford, 1857   *pp.304–305*

John Evelyn on Charles II, 1685:
Thus died King Charles II, of a vigorous and robust constitution, and in all appearances promising a long life. A prince of many virtues, and many great imperfections; debonaire, easy of access, not bloody or cruel; his countenance fierce, his voice great, proper of person, every motion became him; a lover of the sea, and skilful in shipping; not affecting other studies, yet he had a laboratory, and knew of many empirical medicines, and the easier mechanical mathematics; loved planting, building, and brought in a politer way of living, which passed to luxury and intolerable expense. He had a particular talent in telling stories and facetious passages, of which he had innumerable, which made some buffoons and vicious wretches too presumptious and familiar, not worthy the favours they abused. He took delight to have a number of little spaniels to follow him and lie in his bedchamber, where often times he suffered the bitches to puppy and give suck, which rendered it very offensive, and indeed made the whole court nasty and stinking. An excellent prince doubtless, had he been less addicted to women, who made him uneasy and always in want to supply their unmeasureable profusion, and to the detriment of many indigent persons who had signally served both him and his father easily and frequently changed favourites, to his great prejudice, etc. As to other public transactions and unhappy miscarriages, it is not here I intend to number them; but certainly never had king more glorious opportunities to have made himself, his people and all Europe

happy, and prevented innumerable mischiefs, had not his too easy nature resigned him to be managed by crafty men, and some abandoned and profane wretches who corrupted his otherwise sufficient parts, disciplined as he had been by many afflictions during his banishment, which gave him much experience and knowledge of men and things; but those wicked creatures took him off from all application becoming so great a king.

JOHN EVELYN: DIARY, vol. 4
edited by E. S. de Beer   O.U.P., 1955   *pp.409–411*

Thomas Babington, Lord Macaulay, on Charles II:

He had received from nature excellent parts, and a happy temper. His education had been such as might have been expected to develop his understanding, and to form him to the practice of every public and private virtue. He had passed through all varieties of fortune, and had seen both sides of human nature. He had, while very young, been driven forth from a palace, to a life of exile, penury, and danger. He had, at the age when the mind and body are in their highest perfection, and when the first effervescence of boyish passions should have subsided, been recalled from his wanderings to wear a crown. He had been taught by bitter experience how much baseness, perfidy, and ingratitude may lie hid under the obsequious demeanour of courtiers. He had found, on the other hand, in the huts of the poorest, true nobility of soul. When wealth was offered to any who would betray him, when death was denounced against all who should shelter him, cottagers and serving men had kept his secret truly, and had kissed his hand under his mean disguises with as much reverence as if he had been seated on his ancestral throne. From such a school it might have been expected that a young man who wanted neither abilities nor amiable qualities, would have come forth a great and good King. Charles came forth from that school with social habits, with polite and engaging manners, and with some talent for lively conversation, addicted beyond measure to sensual indulgence, fond of sauntering and of frivolous amusements, incapable of selfdenial and of exertion, without faith in human virtue or in human attachment, without desire of renown, and without sensibility to reproach. According to him, every person was to be bought: but some people haggled more about their price than others; and when this haggling was very obstinate and very skilful it was called by some fine name. The chief trick by which clever men kept up the price of their abilities was called integrity. The chief trick by which handsome women kept up the price of their beauty was called modesty. The love of God, the love of country, the love of family, the love of friends, were phrases of the same sort, delicate and convenient synonyms for the love of self. Thinking thus of mankind, Charles naturally cared very little what they thought of him. Honour and shame were scarcely more to him than light and darkness to the blind. His contempt of flattery has been highly commended, but seems, when viewed in connection with the rest of his character, to deserve no commendation. It is possible to be below flattery, as well as above it. One who trusts nobody will not trust sycophants. One who does not value real glory, will not value its counterfeit.

It is creditable to Charles's temper that, ill as he thought of his species, he never became a misanthrope. He saw little in men but what was hateful. Yet he did not hate them. Nay, he was so far humane that it was highly disagreeable to him to see their sufferings or to hear their complaints. This, however, is a sort of humanity which, though amiable and laudable in a private man whose power to help or hurt is bounded by a narrow circle, has in princes often been rather a vice than a virtue. More than one well disposed ruler has given up whole provinces to rapine and oppression, merely from a wish to see none but happy faces round his own board and in his own walks.

THE HISTORY OF ENGLAND FROM THE ACCESSION OF JAMES II, vol. I
by Lord Macaulay, edited by C. H. Firth   Macmillan, 1911 pp.146–147

The next three extracts offer different views of Charles's supposed laziness. The first two authors write as academics; the third, as a popular historian, who, aiming at a wider public, supports the favourable image that most people have of the merry monarch but seeks to refute allegations that have made this image a tarnished one.

David Ogg: a mature judgment:

The King's character is important because his reign was the last but one in English history when a sovereign could himself direct policy. How difficult this was becoming is seen in the short and troubled reign of his brother, James II. Charles's principles of government were personal and even unEnglish, but his successful application of these principles, on the very threshold of modern constitutional sovereignty, shows that he had unusual abilities.... Anxious to secure his own comfort and peace of mind, he took care to avoid challenging or antagonising the nation, and in this way he maintained his personal popularity in England.... Charles, tolerant by nature,... seemed at times to be no more than a spectator.... His success as a king was mainly due not to what he did but to what he refrained from doing, and his posthumous reputation is due almost entirely to a quality rare in kings – an unfailing wit.

CHAMBER'S ENCYCLOPAEDIA, *1967, under 'Charles'*

J. H. Plumb: the view of an up-and-coming historian of the next generation:
> Whatever charm Charles II may have possessed, he certainly lacked, in strong contrast to Louis XIV, single-minded dedication to the business of government. It was the unbuttoned ease, the air of summer relaxation that he brought to the monarchy, rather than his sexual licence, that undermined the awe and respect of his courtiers, servants, and supporters and provided so much grist to his enemies and to those who wished to belittle the monarchy. Can one think of Henry VIII, or even James I, sexually driven as they were, pursuing their lusts in the stews of Covent Garden?
> THE GROWTH OF POLITICAL STABILITY IN ENGLAND, 1675–1725
> *by J. H. Plumb   Macmillan, 1967*   *p.14*

Maurice Ashley:
> ... when one studies Charles's life carefully, it is difficult to point clearly to any occasion when decision was needed or determination had to be shown that he failed to take the necessary action. His mind was quicker than that of most of his advisers, but he was one of those statesmen who are not addicted to paper work. He preferred to reach his conclusions through conversation rather than the study of documents; he loved talking and had an excellent memory; at the same time he was no orator and he kept his speeches, which were usually carefully prepared, short and to the point and thus avoided the blunders sometimes committed by his loquacious grandfather, King James I.... at almost every political crisis of his reign Charles, once he had made up his mind, could not be shaken from his decision. This was particularly true in his relations with the House of Commons. Though constantly pressed to do so, he refused to dismiss the Duke of Lauderdale, who did not give up office until his health broke down. He prevented the Earl of Danby, who had served him loyally, from being impeached for treason and eventually secured his release from imprisonment in the Tower. Unlike his father, Charles was unyielding in upholding his inherited prerogatives: he insisted that it was his sole right to summon, prorogue and dissolve Parliaments; that he alone was entitled to take final decisions on foreign policy; and that he was the authority who directed the movements of the army and navy and controlled the use of the militia. As he himself justly boasted, the older he grew, the firmer he became.
> Charles never at any time lacked courage either as a boy when he was fighting to rescue his father or as a young king in exile, who stood ready to lead the Scots or English into battle to regain his lost thrones; and he died bravely and without complaint. This courage was manifested most clearly during the prolonged exclusion crisis

.... during the twenty-five years of his reign he employed many highly capable men: Clarendon, Arlington, Shaftesbury and Danby were all first-class administrators. Men like Sir William Coventry and Sir Leoline Jenkins were industrious and devoted servants of the Crown. Charles may have been entertained by characters like the second Duke of Buckingham or Charles Berkeley, Lord Falmouth, but he never employed them in really key positions. On the other hand, he came to recognize the conspicuous abilities of Samuel Pepys, who rose from a relatively humble position to become the linchpin of the Admiralty. In General Monck and Prince Rupert he found admirals who served him well within the limits placed upon them. The Earl of Craven proved a trustworthy commander of his small army. Arlington and Sunderland were excellent foreign ministers; Danby and Godolphin were brilliant financiers.

But all these men were his servants. None of them – not even Clarendon – was a Richelieu or a Mazarin.

CHARLES II: THE MAN AND THE STATESMAN
by Maurice Ashley   Weidenfeld & Nicolson, 1971   pp.314–315

Leopold von Ranke, possibly the greatest historian the nineteenth century produced, suggested, on the other hand, that Charles did have at least one political principle. Both von Ranke, however, and the modern American scholar, F. S. Ronalds, who compares Charles with Shaftesbury, would disagree with the view that the King was a statesman.

L. von Ranke, summarizing Charles II's reign:
... he was a thoroughgoing politician. All that he did in his government was founded on the fact, that he could not bring himself to submit to the necessity of being simply a Parliamentary king.

It was a curious combination; on the one hand this Prince, whom nature seemed to have intended for an oriental throne in the middle ages, where he would have played a brilliant part, on the other hand the land of old Germanic freedom, and independent ecclesiastical movement, which had called him back from his exile and then had tried to subject him to the conditions of its old historic life. Against Charles II there arose elements like those to which his father had succumbed: he struggled with them during his whole life, however little it might appear, with skilful energy which grew in stormy times.

A HISTORY OF ENGLAND, vol. 4
by L. von Ranke   O.U.P., 1875   pp.203, 206

F. S. Ronalds:
> ... like a true sportsman Charles had played the game for the sake of the game; he had frustrated the cleverest politician of the seventeenth century in his aspiration to establish the Venetian constitution in England.
>
> THE ATTEMPTED WHIG REVOLUTION OF 1678–1681
>
> *by F. S. Ronalds   New Jersey, 1937*   *p.160*

G. M. Trevelyan, representing the Whig historical tradition, went further and asserted that, after the defeat of the Exclusionists in 1681, Charles lapsed into despotism in fact as well as in intention. This view is based partly on Charles's political actions between 1681 and his death, and partly on the Puritan element in the Whigs which was shocked by Evelyn's description of the King's sexual behaviour. Evelyn, himself inclined to be Puritan, was so impressed by what he saw that he recorded it twice in his diary.

G. M. Trevelyan:
> The second Stuart despotism had come into being. It was based, as Charles had designed in 1670, on a standing army and on the financial help of France. Yet he had realised only half the ideas of the Dover Treaty. For the supreme power which he enjoyed was connected, not with Roman Catholicism and the purchase of Nonconformist support, but with Anglicanism and ferocious persecution of Dissent. The King had bought the Tories at a price. If Charles's successor would continue to pay that price, to extirpate the Nonconformists and depress the Catholics, the despotism wielded in the interest of the squires might be confirmed by time and become the established constitution of the realm. But if an attempt were made to convert it into a Catholic despotism, there would be hope for England yet.
>
> ENGLAND UNDER THE STUARTS
>
> *by G. M. Trevelyan   Methuen, 1920*   *p.425*

John Evelyn, 6 February 1685:
> I am never to forget the inexpressible luxury and profaneness, gaming and all dissolution, and, as it were, total forgetfulness of God (it being Sunday evening) which this day sennight I was witness of: the King sitting and toying with his concubines Portsmouth, Cleveland and Mazarine, etc.; a French boy singing love songs in that glorious gallery; whilst about twenty of the great courtiers and other dissolute persons were at basset round a large table, a bank of at least 2,000 in gold before them; upon which two gentlemen that were with me made reflections with astonishment, it being a scene of utmost vanity, and surely, as they thought, would never have an end. Six days after was all in the dust.
>
> JOHN EVELYN: DIARY, vol. 4
>
> *edited by E. S. de Beer   O.U.P., 1955*   *pp.413–414*

Much more recently, J. P. Kenyon has brought some support, though in a more moderate form, to the view of Evelyn, Burnet and Trevelyan of the old King as a kind of latter-day Tiberius, by making an implicit distinction between the tolerant young man of 1660 and the embittered absolutist of 1685. Hesther Chapman, a popular writer, whose book covers the years before 1660 (with an epilogue to 1685), refuses to make any such distinction.

J. P. Kenyon:

> ... as he watched with impatience the rise of his new palace at Winchester he was heard to remark sombrely that "a year was a great time in his life". The cruelly-exhausting strain of the exclusion crisis, accentuated by illness, had taken a lot out of him. (The wits said he was sexually impotent, a symbolic slander.) He had lost little of his old energy, and he changed little in appearance after 1660, but by 1683 he was a smaller man in ways other than physical. The vicious animosity that had always been a hidden streak in his character was openly displayed in his campaign against the whigs. Even James, the iron man, would listen to those who pleaded for Russell's life, but Charles even brushed aside the intercession of Louis XIV. He told George Legge, "If I do not take his life, he will soon have mine" – the reduction of politics to a personal vendetta. And when every allowance is made for the deficiencies in the seventeenth-century intelligence services and the lack of a police force, the activities of men like Jeffreys, who was appointed Lord Chief Justice in 1683 solely for the terror he could inspire, are a blot on the history of the reign.
>
> THE STUARTS
> *by J. P. Kenyon   Batsford, 1958*   *p.152*

Hesther Chapman:

> ... the apparently triumphant climax of his Restoration does not in fact provide the happy ending such a limitation suggests. The story of his youth is one of moral defeat: the holocaust of a soul. As a boy, he acquired many virtues and most of the graces. By the time he was thirty those graces were greatly enhanced. Of virtue there remained nothing but the façade: a spectral reminder of qualities corrupted and destroyed by disillusion, bitterness, misery and despair.... No inscription, no monument was ordered for the King whose farewell gesture had been that of an affably cynical illusionist.
>
> There was no need of any. His image was not diminished; nor is his power lessened. Still his people find it pleasanter to believe in his half-truths and to be charmed by his jests than to remember how often, and how agreeably, they were deceived.
>
> THE TRAGEDY OF CHARLES II
> *by Hesther Chapman   Cape, 1964*   *pp.13–14, 410*

It takes longer to answer an accusation than to make it. Maurice Ashley on Charles's 'immorality':

> Charles's earlier biographers stressed his personal immorality and suggested that this weakened his capacity to govern. By 'immorality' of course is meant his sexual behaviour. It is not supposed that he drank to excess. Indeed he was often sparse both over food and alcohol, though he enjoyed a good meal and could be mellowed by wine. But nobody has ever been able to make a complete count of his mistresses.... One generation approves the behaviour of King Edward VII; yet in the next, King Edward VIII's love affair cost him his throne. But the only question of real importance is whether such a way of private life damages a statesman's political ability or conduct.... There is no evidence that any of Charles's mistresses when he was a reigning monarch had real influence over his policies. The most they could ever do was to reconcile the King to an erring courtier, as Nell Gwyn did for the Duke of Buckingham. Although Louise de Kéroualle, Charles's most enduring mistress, was first sent to him by Louis XIV of France, she was not even let into all the secrets of Anglo–French relations. Her temporary entry into the camp of the exclusionists did not impress Charles II in the least. It is true that the King sometimes held long conversations with the French ambassador in her apartments, but this was a mere convenience. And if one is to believe, as Charles himself once averred, that he was always fundamentally pro-French at heart, he had attained that attitude of mind long before he ever met the young girl from Brittany. Even when she was firmly established as Duchess of Portsmouth, Louise was never consulted as Louis XIV consulted Madame de Maintenon.... But two things may fairly be pointed out about Charles II and his harem. The first is that it constituted an expensive hobby.... Secondly, Charles's escapades with women did in fact shock members of the older generation, like the first Earl of Clarendon and John Evelyn, even if it did not undermine their loyalty, and can scarcely have endeared the King to the persecuted puritans. But it can have hardly offended Samuel Pepys, whose diary is a well-worn source for criticisms of Charles's weakness (if that is the right word) for women. Pepys had his own enjoyable infidelities. Even John Evelyn had a sanctimonious and repressed love affair with Margaret Blagge, a young Maid of Honour, whose secret marriage to Sidney Godolphin he resented almost as much as Charles II resented the marriage of Frances Stuart. Only a psychoanalyst can measure the unconscious hypocrisies of the human mind.

> If Charles II's mistresses were of relatively small and indirect political importance, Charles's loyalty to his own kindred was immense and significant.
>
> CHARLES II: THE MAN AND THE STATESMAN
> *by Maurice Ashley   Weidenfeld & Nicolson, 1971*   *pp.416–417*

Once again, the popular historian and the academic disagree about Charles. John Bowle presents the popular view of the King's skill in dealing with the political magnates; J. H. Plumb argues that, at least on the local level, Charles failed.

John Bowle:

> That wary cynic, wiliest and most dangerously charming of English kings, was much abler than the lazy lecher of popular belief: early experienced in danger and the shadier side of politics, he was well fitted to deal with the political magnates who now contended for the spoils of office which they considered theirs by right, and to manage his father's enemies who had done well out of the wars.
>
> THE ENGLISH EXPERIENCE
> *by John Bowle   Weidenfeld & Nicolson, 1972*   *p.339*

J. H. Plumb:

> Local royal officials, apart from the Lord-Lieutenants, had become nonentities, and the gentry, as Justices, bore the whole weight of administration. But their power was more extensive than this; they were very largely their own judges and, as Dawson has shown, judicial investigations and decisions that were properly a matter for Chancery were often delegated to them. Of course, they were subject to supervision: first Star Chamber, then Judges on Assize, could belabour them for incompetence, punish them for tyranny, and exhort them on behalf of the Crown. But only Cromwell and Charles II attempted to reduce their power; both failed. By 1688 the gentry were as deeply entrenched in their neighbourhoods as the baronage of Henry III.
>
> The power of the seventeenth-century gentry was sanctioned by violence – riding out against their enemies, hamstringing their neighbour's dogs, beating their farmers' sons, or shooting down their riotous labourers. They played ducks and drakes with the law when it suited them, breaking with impunity what they were supposed to maintain. Since the days of the Tudors no government, royal or republican, had got to terms with them. Like Charles I or Charles II, Cromwell had failed absolutely to take the gentry into his control, and so made Restoration inevitable. Charles II's failure nearly toppled his throne. James II's was more complete; they chased him out of his kingdom.
>
> THE GROWTH OF POLITICAL STABILITY IN ENGLAND, 1675–1725
> *by J. H. Plumb   Macmillan, 1967*   *pp.20–22*

Wooden bust of Charles II by Grinling Gibbons. Crown Copyright – reproduced with permission of the Controller of Her Majesty's Stationery Office.

Statesman or politician? Success or failure? Professor K. H. D. Haley and Christopher Falkus provide us with two contrasting conclusions.

K. H. D. Haley:
> ... in the time of his death he was fortunate. Had he died five years earlier he would have been written off as a failure; had he died five years later his failure to make a positive use of his personal success might have been revealed. As it was, he died in 1685 and was succeeded by a brother whose rapid downfall contrasted sharply with his own peaceful end. But his brother's folly is not a satisfactory reason for exalting Charles. Perhaps the safest conclusion might be that although the graver charges of the Whig historians against him were exaggerated, he cannot convincingly be built up into anything like a great monarch.
>
> CHARLES II
> *by K. H. D. Haley   The Historical Association, 1966*   p.22

Christopher Falkus:
> But when everything is said, Charles's achievement remains. Alone among the Stuarts he retained the common touch. Where men of high principle – his father, brother, and Oliver Cromwell among them – opened wounds, Charles, in his very personal way, was able to bide his time and wait. To a degree he succeeded where a greater or a lesser man would have failed. Perhaps it was as well that between the violence of civil war and the catastrophe of the reign of James II England had the prince described by Halifax, who 'might more properly be said to have gifts than virtues, as affability, easiness of living', and, most important of all, 'inclinations to give and to forgive'.
>
> CHARLES II
> *by Christopher Falkus   Weidenfeld & Nicolson, 1972*   p.216

Further Reading

Maurice Ashley *Charles II: The Man and the Statesman* (WEIDENFELD & NICOLSON, 1971)
Andrew Browning (editor) *English Historical Documents*, vol. 8 *(1660–1714)* (EYRE & SPOTTISWOODE, 1953)
Andrew Browning *Thomas Osborne, Earl of Danby and Duke of Leeds, 1632–1712: Life and Letters (3 vols.)* (JACKSON, SON & CO., GLASGOW, 1951)
Sir Arthur Bryant *King Charles II* (COLLINS, 1955)
Sir Arthur Bryant (editor) *Letters, Speeches and Declarations of King Charles II* (CASSELL, 1935)
Gilbert Burnet *History of My Own Time (edited by O. Airy) (2 vols.)* (O.U.P., 1897–1900)
Hesther Chapman *The Tragedy of Charles II* (CAPE, 1965)
G. R. Cragg *Puritanism in the Period of the Great Persecution, 1660–1688* (C.U.P., 1957)
John Dryden *Poems (edited by James Kinsley) (4 vols.)* (O.U.P., 1958)
John Evelyn *Diary (edited by E. S. de Beer)* (O.U.P., 1955)
Christopher Falkus *The Life and Times of Charles II* (WEIDENFELD & NICOLSON, 1972)
Graham Greene *Lord Rochester's Monkey* (BODLEY HEAD, 1974)
K. H. D. Haley *Charles II* (THE HISTORICAL ASSOCIATION, 1966)
K. H. D. Haley *The First Earl of Shaftesbury* (O.U.P., 1968)
G. M. D. Howat *Stuart and Cromwellian Foreign Policy* (A & C BLACK, 1974)
James Rees Jones *The First Whigs: The Politics of the Exclusion Crisis, 1678–1683* (O.U.P., 1961)
J. P. Kenyon *The Stuarts* (BATSFORD, 1958)
J. P. Kenyon *Robert Spencer, Earl of Sunderland, 1641–1702* (LONGMANS, 1958)
J. P. Kenyon *The Stuart Constitution, 1603–1688* (C.U.P., 1966)
J. P. Kenyon *The Popish Plot* (HEINEMANN, 1972)
Maurice Lee *The Cabal* (UNIV. OF ILLINOIS PRESS, 1965)

David Lunn 'Father John Hudleston and Charles II' (*HISTORY TODAY*, April 1975, vol. 25, pp.229–237)
Lord Macaulay *The History of England from the Accession of James II (edited by C. H. Firth) (6 vols.)* (MACMILLAN, 1911)
John Miller *Popery and Politics in England, 1660–1688* (C.U.P., 1973)
David Ogg *England in the Reign of Charles II (second edition, 2 vols.)* (O.U.P., 1963)
J. H. Plumb *The Growth of Political Stability in England, 1675–1725* (MACMILLAN, 1967)
James Sutherland *English Literature and the Late Seventeenth Century* (O.U.P., 1969)
Joan Thirsk *The Restoration* (LONGMAN, 1976)
F. C. Turner *James II* (EYRE & SPOTTISWOODE, 1948)
L. von Ranke *A History of England (5 vols.)* (O.U.P., 1875)
Anne Whiteman *From Uniformity to Unity, 1662–1962 (edited by G. F. Nuttall and O. Chadwick)* (S.P.C.K., 1962)
Charles H. Wilson *England's Apprenticeship, 1603–1763* (LONGMANS, 1965)
D. T. Witcombe *Charles II and the Cavalier House of Commons, 1660–1674* (MANCHESTER U.P., 1966)

Acknowledgments and Sources

Bust of Charles II by Honoré Pellé. *The Victoria and Albert Museum.* — *page 3*

Detail from *Charles II's Coronation Procession* by Dirck Stoop. *Roy Miles Fine Paintings, 6 Duke Street, St James's, London SW1.* — *page 5*

John Wilmot, 2nd Earl of Rochester by Jacob Huysmans. *Print supplied by the Royal Academy of Arts; reproduced by kind permission of Lord Brooke.* — *page 6*

Edward Hyde, Earl of Clarendon. *Reproduced by permission of the Courtauld Institute of Art and the Benchers of the Honourable Society of the Middle Temple.* — *page 9*

Whitehall Palace by Visscher. *Reproduced by Courtesy of the Trustees of the British Museum.* — *page 16*

The Princess Henrietta, attributable to Sir Peter Lely. *Exeter Museums Service.* — *page 19*

Louis XIV and Charles II. *Reproduced by Courtesy of the Trustees of the British Museum.* — *page 25*

Thomas Osborne, Earl of Danby. *National Portrait Gallery, London.* — *page 30*

Extract from *ENGLISH HISTORICAL REVIEW. Longman Group Ltd.* — *page 32*

Titus Oates, inventor of the 'Popish Plot'. *The Mansell Collection.* — *page 33*

James, Duke of York. *Reproduced by gracious permission of Her Majesty the Queen.* — *page 35*

Babel and Bethel. *Reproduced by Courtesy of the Trustees of the British Museum.* — *page 39*

page 55	Tangiers from the South West. *Reproduced by Courtesy of the Trustees of the British Museum.*
page 59	Samuel Pepys. *National Portrait Gallery, London.*
page 63	The Royal Chapel, Windsor Castle. *Reproduced by gracious permission of Her Majesty the Queen.*
page 65	Tennis Match. *Radio Times Hulton Picture Library.*
page 65	Pall Mall. *The Mansell Collection.*
page 69	John Dryden. *Radio Times Hulton Picture Library.*
page 71	The Castlemaine Globe. *Whipple Museum of the History of Science, Cambridge.*
page 72	Charles II and the Royal Society. *Science Museum, London.*
page 73	*Entrance to the Fleet River* by Samuel Scott. *Guildhall Library, City of London.*
pages 81 and 85	Extracts from *Charles II: The Man and the Statesman* by Maurice Ashley. *Weidenfeld and Nicolson.*
page 87	Wooden head of Charles II. *Crown Copyright – reproduced with permission of the Controller of Her Majesty's Stationery Office.*